# Thermal Analysis with SOLIDWORKS Simulation 2015 and Flow Simulation 2015

## Paul M. Kurowski, Ph.D., P.Eng.

CERTIFIED
Solution
Partner

DS SOLIDWORKS

SDC
Publications

Design Generator, Inc.

**SDC Publications**
P.O. Box 1334
Mission, KS 66222
913-262-2664
www.SDCpublications.com
Publisher: Stephen Schroff

**Trademarks and Disclaimer**

SOLIDWORKS® is a registered trademark of Dassault Systémes SolidWorks Corp.

Microsoft Windows® and its family products are registered trademarks of the Microsoft Corporation.

Every effort has been made to provide an accurate text. The author and the manufacturers shall not be held liable for any parts or products developed with this book or held responsible for any inaccuracies or errors that appear in the book

**About the Cover**
The image on the cover shows temperature results of analysis of the radiator 2015PART model. This model can be found in downloadable exercises, chapter 18. It comes with Simulation studies defined.

ISBN-13: 978-1-58503-939-5
ISBN-10: 1-58503-939-X

Printed and bound in the United States of America.

# *About the Author*

Dr. Paul Kurowski obtained his M.Sc. and Ph.D. in Applied Mechanics from Warsaw Technical University. He completed postdoctoral work at Kyoto University. Dr. Kurowski is an Assistant Professor in the Department of Mechanical and Materials Engineering, at the University of Western Ontario. His teaching includes Finite Element Analysis, Product Design, Kinematics and Dynamics of Machines and Mechanical Vibrations. His interests focus on Computer Aided Engineering methods used as tools of product design.

Dr. Kurowski is also the President of Design Generator Inc., a consulting firm with expertise in Product Development, Design Analysis, and training in Computer Aided Engineering.

Dr. Kurowski has published many technical papers and taught professional development seminars for the Society of Automotive Engineers (SAE), the American Society of Mechanical Engineers (ASME), the Association of Professional Engineers of Ontario (PEO), the Parametric Technology Corporation (PTC), Rand Worldwide, SOLIDWORKS Corporation and others.

Dr. Kurowski is a member of the Association of Professional Engineers of Ontario and the Society of Automotive Engineers. He can be contacted at www.designgenerator.com

# *Acknowledgements*

I would like to thank the students attending my various courses for their valuable comments and questions. I would like to thank Tom Kurowski for editing the text and the exercises. I thank my wife Elżbieta for formatting, proof reading and project management support.


Paul Kurowski

# Table of contents

# Exercise Files

To download the files that are required for this book, type the following in the address bar of your web browser:

**SDCpublications.com/downloads/978-1-58503-939-5**

# Before You Start

## *Notes on hands-on exercises and functionality of Simulation*

This book goes beyond a standard software manual. It takes a unique approach by bridging the theory of heat transfer with examples showing the practical implementation of thermal analysis. This book builds on material covered in **"Engineering Analysis with SOLIDWORKS Simulation 2014."**

We recommend that you study the exercises in the order presented in the book. As you go through the exercises, you will notice that explanations and steps described in detail in earlier exercises are not repeated in later chapters. Each subsequent exercise assumes familiarity with software functions discussed in previous exercises and builds on the skills, experience, and understanding gained from previously presented problems. Exceptions to this sequential approach are chapters 14, 15, 16 where **Flow Simulation** is used. These chapters may be skipped by readers not interested in problems involving **Flow Simulation**.

The functionality of **SOLIDWORKS Simulation** depends on which software **Simulation** product is used.

Exercises in this book require different levels of **SOLIDWORKS Simulation** functionality and this depends on which Simulation product is used. The **SOLIDWORKS Simulation** Product Matrix document is available at:

http://www.SOLIDWORKS.com/sw/products/simulation/simulation-matrices.htm

All exercises in this book use **SOLIDWORKS** models, which can be downloaded from www.SDCpublications.com. Most exercises do not contain any **Simulation** studies; you are expected to create all studies, results plots, and graphs yourself. The only exception is the cover page part model RADIATOR 2015 which comes with all studies defined. All problems presented here have been solved with **SOLIDWORKS Simulation Premium** running on Windows 7 in a 64 bit operating environment.

Working on exercises you may notice that your results may be slightly different from results presented in this book. This is because numerical results may differ slightly depending on the operating system and software service pack.

We encourage you to explore each exercise beyond its description by investigating other options, other menu choices, and other ways to present results. You will soon discover that the same simple logic applies to all functions in **SOLIDWORKS Simulation**, be it structural or thermal analysis.

This book is not intended to replace software manuals. Therefore, not all Thermal Analysis capabilities with **Simulation** are covered. The knowledge acquired by the reader will not be strictly software specifics. The same concepts, tools and methods apply to any FEA software.

## *Prerequisites*

"**Thermal Analysis with SOLIDWORKS Simulation**" is not an introductory text to **SOLIDWORKS Simulation**. Rather, it picks up Thermal Analysis from where it was left in the pre-requisite textbook "**Engineering Analysis with SOLIDWORKS Simulation.**" If you are new to **SOLIDWORKS Simulation** we recommend to use "**Engineering Analysis with SOLIDWORKS Simulation**" to gain essential familiarity with Finite Element Analysis. At the very least go through chapters 1, 2, 3, 7, 8, 10 of that pre-requisite textbook.

The following prerequisites are recommended:

- ❑ An understanding of Heat Transfer Analysis
- ❑ An understanding of Structural Analysis
- ❑ An understanding of Solid Mechanics
- ❑ Familiarity with **SOLIDWORKS Simulation** to the extent covered in "**Engineering Analysis with SOLIDWORKS Simulation**" or equivalent experience
- ❑ Familiarity with the Windows Operating System

## *Selected terminology*

The mouse pointer plays a very important role in executing various commands and providing user feedback. The mouse pointer is used to execute commands, select geometry, and invoke pop-up menus. We use Windows terminology when referring to mouse-pointer actions.

| Item | Description |
|------|-------------|
| **Click** | Self-explanatory |
| **Double-click** | Self-explanatory |
| **Click-inside** | Click the left mouse button. Wait a second, and then click the left mouse button inside the pop-up menu or text box. Use this technique to modify the names of folders and icons in **SOLIDWORKS Simulation** Manager. |
| **Drag and drop** | Use the mouse to point to an object. Press and hold the left mouse button down. Move the mouse pointer to a new location. Release the left mouse button. |
| **Right-click** | Click the right mouse button. A pop-up menu is displayed. Use the left mouse button to select a desired menu command. |

All **SOLIDWORKS** file names appear in CAPITAL letters, even though the actual file names may use a combination of capital and small letters. Selected menu items and **SOLIDWORKS Simulation** commands appear in **bold**, **SOLIDWORKS** configurations, **SOLIDWORKS Simulation** folders, icon names and study names appear in *italics* except in captions and comments to illustrations. **SOLIDWORKS** and **Simulation** also appear in bold font. Bold font may also be used to draw reader's attention to a particular term.

# 1: Introduction

## *Topics covered*

- ❏ Heat transfer by conduction
- ❏ Heat transfer by convection
- ❏ Heat transfer by radiation
- ❏ Thermal boundary conditions
- ❏ Analogies between thermal and structural analysis
- ❏ Thermal elements: solids and shells
- ❏ Scalar and vector entities, presenting results
- ❏ Steady state thermal analysis
- ❏ Transient thermal analysis
- ❏ Linear thermal analysis
- ❏ Nonlinear thermal analysis

## *What is Thermal Analysis?*

Thermal analysis deals with heat transfer in solid bodies. We approach thermal analysis from the perspective of a user experienced in structural analysis such as static, modal, buckling etc. as implemented in **SOLIDWORKS Simulation**. You will soon notice that experience in structural analysis is directly transferable to thermal analysis because of the close analogies between structural and thermal analyses. The temperature is analogous to displacement in structural analysis, strain to temperature gradient, and stress to heat flux. Selected analogies are summarized in Figure 1-1.

| Structural Analysis | Thermal Analysis |
|---|---|
| Displacement [m] | Temperature [K] |
| Strain [1] | Temperature gradient [K/m] |
| Stress [N/m²] | Heat flux [W/m²] |
| Load [N] [N/m] [N/m²] [N/m³] | Heat source [W] [W/m] [W/m²] [W/m³] |
| Prescribed displacement [m] | Prescribed temperature [K] |
| Pressure [N/m²] | Prescribed heat flux [W/m²] |
| Hook's law: $$\sigma = E\frac{du}{dx}$$ | Fourier's law: $$q = -k\frac{dT}{dx}$$ |
| Stiffness matrix | Conductivity matrix |

Figure 1-1: Analogies between structural and thermal analyses with units in SI system.

*Different system of units may be used except for radiation problems where temperature is absolute and must be expressed in Kelvins.*

The primary unknown in structural analysis is displacement; the primary unknown in thermal analysis is temperature. This leads to an important difference between structural and thermal analysis performed with the finite element method. Displacement, which is a vector and includes both translation and rotation, requires up to six degrees of freedom per node. The number of degrees of freedom in structural analysis depends on the type of elements; for example, solid elements have three degrees of freedom and shell elements have six degrees of freedom per node. Two dimensional structural elements have two degrees of freedom per node. Temperature is a scalar and requires only one degree of freedom per node, regardless of element type. This makes thermal problems much easier to solve because thermal models typically have fewer degrees of freedom as compared to structural models.

Another conceptual difference is that thermal analysis is never a "static" analysis. If heat flow does not change, then the problem is "steady state analysis" and not static because heat flow never stops. If heat flow changes with time, then the problem is called transient.

## *Mechanisms of heat transfer*

### Conduction

In a solid body, the energy is transferred from a high temperature region to a low temperature region. The rate of heat transfer per unit area is proportional to the material thermal conductivity, cross sectional area and temperature gradient in the normal direction; it is inversely proportional to the distance (Figure 1-2). This mode of heat transfer is referred to as conduction:

$$Q_{COND} = kA(T_{HOT} - T_{COLD})/L$$

Where:

$Q_{COND}$ – Heat transferred by conduction [W]

k – Thermal conductivity [W/m/K]

$A$ – Cross sectional area [m$^2$]

$T_{HOT}$ – Temperature on the hot side [K]

$T_{COLD}$ – Temperature on the cold side [K]

$L$ – Distance of heat travel [m]

Conduction is responsible for heat transfer inside a solid body.

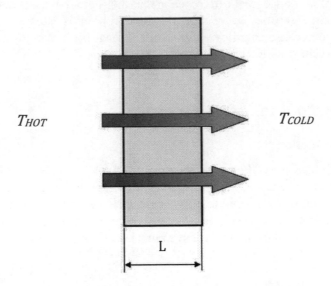

<u>Figure 1-2: Heat transfer by conduction.</u>

*Conduction is responsible for heat transfer inside a solid body.*

Thermal conductivity is vastly different for different materials as shown in Figure 1-3.

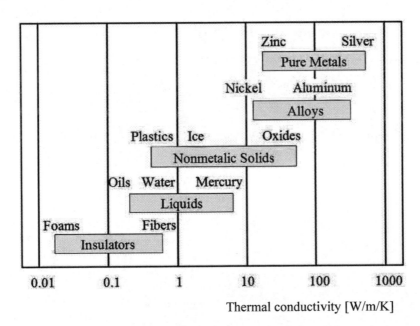

<u>Figure 1-3: Thermal conductivity for different materials.</u>

*There are five orders of magnitude difference in thermal conductivity between the best conductors and best insulators.*

**Convection**

Convective heat transfer is the heat flow between a solid body and the surrounding fluid (either liquid or gas). Convective heat transfer can be either natural convection where the fluid flow is due to the variation in specific weight of a hot and cold fluid, or forced convection where the fluid is forced to flow past the solid body. Therefore, natural convection requires gravity (Figure 1-4), and forced convection does not require gravity (Figure 1-5). Since fluid (air, water, steam, oil etc.) is required for heat transfer by convection, this type of heat transfer cannot happen in a vacuum. Heat exchanged by convection is expressed as:

$$Q_{CONV} = hA(T_S - T_F)$$

Where:

$Q_{CONV}$ – Heat transferred by convection [W]

$h$ – Convection coefficient [W/m²/K]

$A$ – Surface area [m²]

$T_S$ – Surface temperature [K]

$T_F$ - Fluid bulk temperature [K]

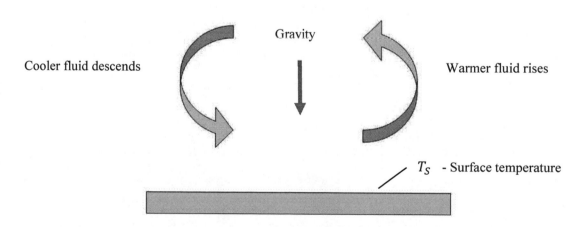

$T_F$ - Bulk temperature of fluid in contact with surface

Gravity

Cooler fluid descends

Warmer fluid rises

$T_S$ - Surface temperature

Figure 1-4: Heat transfer by natural convection.

*Convective heat transfer can take place only in the presence of fluid and gravity.*

Figure 1-5: Natural and forced convection.

*Forced convection doesn't require gravity.*

The magnitude of the convection coefficient strongly depends on the medium (fluid) surrounding a solid body (Figure1-6).

| Medium | Convection coefficient $W/m^2/K$ |
|---|---|
| Air (natural convection) | 5-25 |
| Air/superheated steam | 20-300 |
| Oil (forced convection) | 60-1800 |
| Water (forced convection) | 300-6000 |
| Water (boiling) | 3000-60000 |
| Steam (condensing) | 6000-120000 |

Figure 1-6: Convection coefficient for different media.

*There are five orders of difference in convection coefficients between different media and different types of convection.*

**Radiation**

Radiation heat transfer occurs between a solid body and the ambient or between two solid bodies without presence of any medium (fluid). This is the only type of heat transfer that occurs in a vacuum. Heat flows by electromagnetic radiation. The upper limit to the emissive power is a back body radiating heat and is prescribed by the Stefan-Boltzmann law:

$$q = \sigma T_s^4$$

Where:

$q$ – Heat flux (heat emitted by radiation per unit of area) [W/m$^2$]

$\sigma$ – Stefan-Boltzmann constant = 5.67x10$^{-9}$ [W/m$^2$/K$^4$]

$T_s$ – Surface temperature [K]

The heat flux emitted by a real surface is less than that of a black body at the same temperature. It is given as:

$$q = \varepsilon \sigma T_s^4$$

where $\varepsilon$ is a radiative property of a surface called emissivity. Values of $\varepsilon$ are in the range of $0 \leq \varepsilon \leq 1$ and provide a measure of how well the surface emits radiative energy in comparison to a black body. It depends strongly on the surface material and finish. For example, a polished aluminum surface has an emissivity of about 0.05; an oxidized aluminum surface has an emissivity of 0.25. The emissivity also depends on the temperature of the face emitting heat by radiation.

In heat transfer by radiation, heat may be radiated out to space by a single body; it may be exchanged between two bodies or it may be exchanged between two bodies as well as radiated out to space (Figure 1-7).

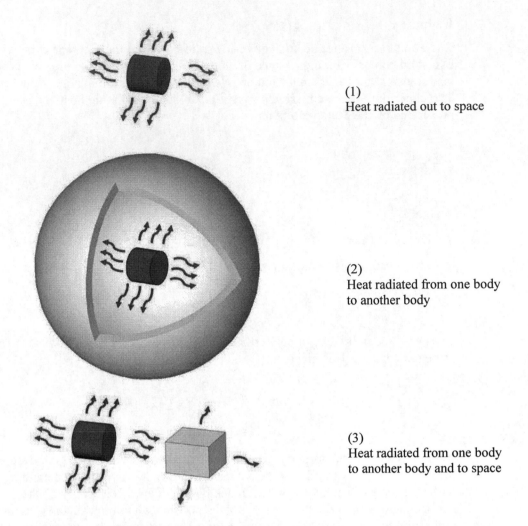

(1)
Heat radiated out to space

(2)
Heat radiated from one body
to another body

(3)
Heat radiated from one body
to another body and to space

Figure 1-7: Different cases of heat transfer by radiation.

*If heat is exchanged between two bodies only and not radiated out to space, then one body must be fully enclosed by the other body (2). Heat gained by radiation may be radiated out again into space (3).*

Having introduced three mechanisms of heat transfer we need to make a very important statement. With **SOLIDWORKS Simulation** which uses the finite element method, only heat transfer by conduction is modeled directly. Convection and radiation are modeled as boundary conditions. This is done by defining convection and/or radiation coefficients to faces that participate in heat exchange between the model and the environment.

The next two examples show how a prescribed temperature, convection and heat load work together to induce heat flow inside a solid body. These examples are not hands-on exercises. Hands-on exercises will start in chapter 2.

## Heat Flow Induced By Prescribed Temperatures

Just like stresses may be caused by prescribed displacement, heat flow may be induced by temperature differences defined by prescribed temperatures. Consider the model BRACKET TH with different temperatures defined on two faces as shown in Figure 1-8. Note that the temperature field establishes itself in the model but heat flow continues due to temperature gradients. Also notice that no heat escapes from the model because we have not defined any mechanism to exchange heat through any surfaces other than the two faces with prescribed temperatures. This implies that the model is perfectly insulated, except for two faces where prescribed temperatures are defined and may correspond to a situation where the bracket holding a hot pipe is mounted on a cold surface and heat escaping through faces exposed to air is negligible.

Figure 1-8: Temperature distribution in the model where heat flow is induced by prescribed temperatures.

*A temperature of 300°C is applied to the cylindrical face, and a temperature of 20°C is applied to the back face.*

Plot in Figure 1-8 uses custom colors (grey substituted for blue) to improve black and white print quality. Custom colors will be used frequently to present fringe plots in this book. Custom colors may be defined in **Chart Options** in plot settings.

## *Heat flow induced by heat load and convection*

Heat flow can also be induced by the applied heat load. The unit of heat load applied to a surface is called heat flux; heat flowing through an imaginary cross-section is also called heat flux. Total heat applied to a volume or face is called heat power. Notice that since thermal analysis deals with heat flow, a mechanism for that heat flow to occur must be in place. In the heat sink problem HEAT SINK01, shown in Figure 1-9, heat enters the radiator model through the base, as defined by the applied heat power which is a close analogy to force load in structural analysis. Convection coefficients [W/m²/K], also called film coefficients, are defined for all remaining surfaces and provide the way to remove heat from the model. Heat enters the model through the base where heat power is defined. Heat escapes the model through faces where convection coefficients are defined.

Heat power
on this face

Temperature plot                    Heat flux plot

<u>Figure 1-9: Temperature distribution and heat flux in a heat sink model.</u>

*A temperature plot being a scalar quantity can only be shown using a fringe display. Heat flux is a vector quantity and can be illustrated either by a fringe plot or vector plot. Notice that arrows "coming out" of the walls illustrate heat that escapes the model because of convection.*

The structural analogy of convection coefficients is a bit less intuitive. Convection coefficients are analogous to elastic support offered by distributed springs. Just like supports and/or prescribed displacements are necessary to establish model equilibrium in a structural analysis problem, convection coefficients and/or prescribed temperatures are necessary to establish heat flow in a thermal analysis problem. Indeed, an attempt to run thermal analysis with heat loads but with no convection coefficients or prescribed temperatures results in an error similar to the one caused by the absence of supports in structural analysis.

## Modeling considerations in thermal analysis

Symmetry boundary conditions can be used in thermal analysis based on the observation that if symmetry exists in both geometry and boundary conditions, then there is no heat flowing through a plane of symmetry. After simplifying the model to ½ in case of single symmetry or to ¼ in case of double symmetry (Figure 1-10), nothing needs to be done to surfaces exposed by cuts. No convection coefficients defined for those surfaces means that no heat flows across them.

Full model                           ¼ model

Figure 1-10: Model DOUBLE SYM with double symmetry can be simplified to ¼ of its size.

*No thermal boundary conditions are applied to faces in the plane of symmetry.*

Axisymmetric problems may be represented by 2D models as shown in Figure 1-11.

Axis of symmetry

Full model                    2D cross section along the axis of symmetry

Figure 1-11: Axisymmetric model AXISYM represented by a 2D cross section.

Notice that models DOUBLE SYM (Figure 1-10) and AXISYM (Figure 1-11) are suitable for analysis of temperature, but because of sharp re-entrant edges, they are not suitable for analysis of heat flux in the vicinity of the sharp re-entrant edges because heat flux there is singular. This is in direct analogy to sharp re-entrant edges causing stress singularities in structural models.

Once you acquire sufficient familiarity with thermal analysis you are encouraged to analyze models BRACKET TH, HEAT SINK01, DOUBLE SYM and AXISYM using thermal parameters of your choice.

Let's wrap up this review with an important observation which will serve as a guide to all thermal analysis problems. In structural analysis we define a load path by defining loads and supports. In a heat transfer problem, we define a mechanism of heat transfer; we must know how heat enters the model, how it travels through the model and how it exits the model.

## *Types of thermal analysis*

Thermal analysis may be linear or nonlinear, steady state or time-dependent as shown in Figure 1-12.

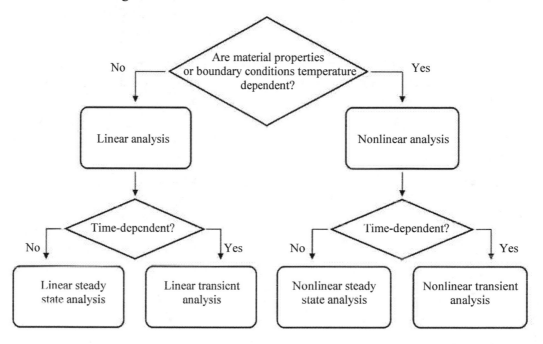

Figure 1-12: Types of thermal analyses.

In linear analysis, the conductivity matrix does not change during the solution process; in nonlinear analysis it must be modified because material properties and/or boundary conditions are temperature dependent. In steady state analysis, material conditions and boundary conditions do not change with time; in time dependent (transient) they do change.

We will be working with all of types of thermal analyses shown in Figure 1-12.

## Thermal analysis with SOLIDWORKS Simulation

**SOLIDWORKS Simulation** uses methods of finite element analysis to solve both structural and thermal problems. CAD models prepared in **SOLIDWORKS** are discretized (meshed) into finite elements. The elements' type depends on the type of geometry prepared in **SOLIDWORKS**. Solid bodies are meshed into solid elements; Surface bodies are meshed into shell elements; 2D axisymmetric and extruded models are meshed into corresponding 2D elements. Types of finite elements, meshing techniques and other mesh specific considerations are discussed in details in the pre-requisite text "**Engineering Analysis with SOLIDWORKS Simulation.**" Here we limit our review to thermal analysis specific issues.

Elements available in thermal analysis with **SOLIDWORKS Simulation** are shown in Figure 1-13. Notice that beam elements are not available in thermal analysis.

| | 3D elements | | 2D elements |
|---|---|---|---|
| | **Solid elements** | **Shell elements** | **Axisymmetric elements**<br><br>**Extruded elements** |
| **First order element**<br><br>Linear (first order) temperature field<br><br>Constant heat flux field | | | |
| **Second order element**<br><br>Parabolic (second order) temperature field<br><br>Linear heat flux field | | | |

Figure 1-13: Elements available in thermal analysis with SOLIDWORKS Simulation.

*The majority of analyses use the second order tetrahedral element.*

First order elements do not offer any advantages in either structural or thermal analysis and beam elements are neither applicable nor available in thermal analysis. Therefore we are left with second order solids and second order shells to model 3D problems and second order plate elements to model 2D axisymmetric or extruded problems.

Prior to commencing work with thermal problems, make sure that **Solid Bodies** and **Surface Bodies** are visible in the **SOLIDWORKS** Feature Manager (Figure 1-14).

Figure 1-14: Settings of Feature Manager.

*To facilitate working with Simulation models make sure that Solid Bodies and Surface Bodies are always visible.*

*Notes:*

# 2: Hollow plate

## *Topics covered*

- ❑  Heat transfer by conduction
- ❑  Heat transfer by convection
- ❑  Different ways of presenting results of thermal analysis
- ❑  Convergence analysis in thermal problems
- ❑  Solid elements in heat transfer problems
- ❑  Shell elements in heat transfer problems

## *Project description*

We'll conduct thermal analysis of simple models to study the effects of discretization error and the use of different types of elements. In this chapter we use our expertise in structural analysis gained from "**Engineering Analysis with SOLIDWORKS Simulation.**" We use HOLLOW PLATE TH, similar to the model from this introductory textbook where it is used in structural analysis examples.

Open model HOLLOW PLATE TH and review the two configurations: *01 solid* where the model is represented as a solid body and *02 shell* where the model is represented as a surface body. Stay in the *01 solid* configuration and create a thermal study called *01 solid*. Apply the prescribed temperature boundary conditions as shown in Figure 2-1; these prescribed temperatures will induce heat flow from hot to cold.

Hot side 400K                                    Cold side 300K

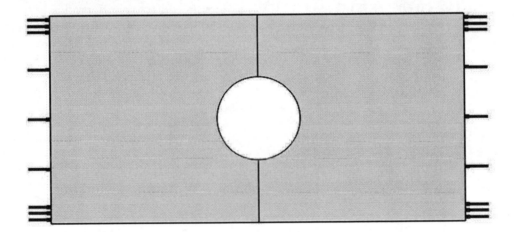

Figure 2-1: Prescribed temperatures boundary conditions applied to two end faces.

*No convection is defined anywhere in the model meaning that all faces are insulated except where temperature boundary conditions are defined.*

Repeat the definition of the prescribed temperature on the hot side where it is 400K. Mesh the model with a coarse mesh as shown in Figure 2-2.

Figure 2-2: Coarse mesh created with 15mm element size.

*Use Standard mesh; do not use Draft quality elements. This mesh is coarse; it is used only as the first step in the convergence process.*

Run the solution and create two plots: **Temperature** and **Resultant Heat Flux**, probe results as shown in Figure 2-3 and Figure 2-4.

Figure 2-3: Temperature results: 350K in the probed location.

*Probe at the vertex created by the split line.*

Figure 2-4: Resultant heat flux results: 189902W/m² in the probed location.

*Probe at the vertex created by the split line. Your result may be slightly different depending on the solver and service pack used. This applies to all Simulation results presented in this book.*

Repeat the analysis using a mesh of default size 5.72mm (study *02 solid*) and a fine mesh with element size 2mm (study *03 solid*). Optionally try meshing the model with 1mm element size but be prepared for a long run. Notice that while temperature results are almost insensitive to mesh refinement, the resultant heat flux changes with mesh refinement as shown in Figure 2-5.

Figure 2-5: Resultant heat flux in the probed location as a function of the inverse of element size.

*Four points are connected by line only to visually enhance the graph.*

As the graph in Figure 2-5 demonstrates, the heat flux converges to a finite value and the default element size produces acceptable results. What should also be noticed is that every given mesh introduces artificial thermal resistance; the coarser the mesh the larger that added resistance is and that causes lower heat flux. This is the effect of discretization error in direct analogy to structural models where artificial stiffness is added to the model by discretization (meshing).

Copy study *02 solid* (the one with default mesh) into study *05 solid convection*. We'll use it to demonstrate convective heat transfer out of the plate. Delete prescribed temperature on the cold size. In its place define **Convection** as shown in Figure 2-6.

Convection coefficient ———

Temperature of
surrounding air ———

Figure 2-6: Definition of convection on ½ of one side.

*As always, definition of convection requires a convection coefficient and bulk temperature which is the temperature of the fluid surrounding the model.*

*A convection coefficient of 50W/m²/K corresponds to free convection with air.*

Run the solution of study *05 solid convection* and obtain results as shown in Figure 2-7.

Temperature

Heat flux

Figure 2-7: Temperature and heat flux results in the presence of convection.

*Temperature is a scalar value and can only be plotted using fringe plots as shown above. Heat flux is a vector value; presenting it as a fringe plot shows only the magnitude but not the direction of heat flow.*

Modify the heat flux plot into a vector plot as shown in Figure 2-8.

Figure 2-8: Heat flux results presented as a vector plot display the direction of heat flow.

*Rotate the plot as required to see vectors "coming out" of the model through the face where convection conditions have been defined.*

You may want to review the results of other studies with heat flux results shown as a vector plot.

Having demonstrated analogies between the convergence process in structural and thermal analyses using solid elements, we'll now study the use of shell element in thermal analysis.

Stay with model HOLLOW PLATE TH but switch to *02 surface* configuration. Create a thermal study *06 surface convection*. Define the surface thickness as shown in Figure 2-9.

Figure 2-9: Definition of surface thickness.

*The definition of thickness is required because thickness is not specified in the surface CAD model. Thermal analysis does not distinguish between Thin and Thick shell element formulation.*

Follow steps in Figure 2-10 to eliminate the **Solid Body** from the analysis.

Right-click
Solid Body
Select
Exclude from Analysis

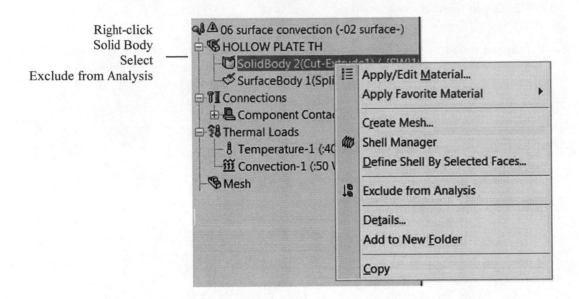

Figure 2-10: Exclusion of the Solid Body from the analysis.

*Even though the Solid Body was made invisible in the CAD model, it still forms a part of the CAD geometry and needs to be excluded from the analysis.*

Apply thermal boundary conditions as in study *05 solid convection*: a prescribed temperature of 400K on the hot side (the edge) and convection to the side face as shown in Figure 2-6. Use the default element size to mesh the model into shell elements, obtain a solution and present **Temperature** and **Heat Flux** results using fringe plots (Figure 2-11).

Figure 2-11: Temperature and heat flux results from the shell element model presented as fringe plots.

*These results are very similar to the results produced by the solid element model.*

While fringe plots show little difference between results obtained from the solid element and shell element models, vector plots do show important differences (Figure 2-12).

Figure 2-12: Heat flux results in the shell element model presented with vector plots.

*Rotate the plot to see that heat flux vectors do not "come out" of the model.*

In structural analysis shell elements differentiate between top and bottom and different stress results are read on opposite sides. In thermal analysis shell elements do not differentiate between sides. Therefore, the shell element model cannot show to which side heat escapes from the model. As shown in Figure 2-12, heat flux vectors "fade away" without "coming out" of the model.

Since in thermal analysis shell elements do not differentiate between sides, you cannot apply different thermal boundary conditions to the sides of face meshed with shell elements.

# 3: L bracket

## *Topics covered*

- ❑ Heat transfer by conduction
- ❑ Use of 2D models
- ❑ Singularities in thermal problems

## *Project description*

We'll conduct a thermal analysis of a simple model to study heat flux singularities. Demonstration of heat flux singularities requires the use of very small elements; consequently, models are large and expensive to solve. However, our model lends itself toward a 2D representation. Using 2D thermal elements, we'll demonstrate a heat flux singularity at a fraction of the computational effort that would be required if a 3D analysis were performed.

Open model L BRACKET TH shown in Figure 3-1; make sure it is in the *01 sharp edge* configuration.

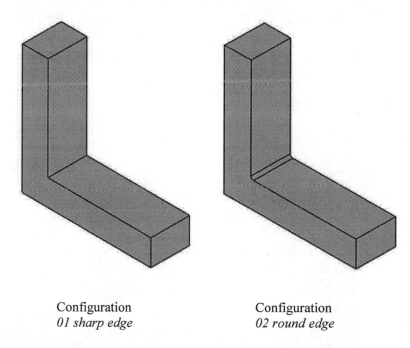

Configuration
*01 sharp edge*

Configuration
*02 round edge*

Figure 3-1: Model L BRACKET TH comes in two configurations: one with a sharp edge and one with a round edge.

*Demonstrating heat flux singularities requires a model with a sharp edge.*

Create a thermal study *01 sharp* using 2D Simplification (Figure 3-2).

3D CAD geometry

2D analysis geometry

Figure 3-2: Model L BRACKET TH can be represented by a 2D section.

*Section depth is the thickness of the CAD model.*

To demonstrate the heat flux singularity we must define heat flow in the model. The easiest way to do that is to define prescribed temperatures as boundary conditions as shown in Figure 3-3.

Figure 3-3: Definition of prescribed temperatures in 2D thermal model; top edge: 400K, right edge: 200K.

*The temperature window shows the definition of a 200K prescribed temperature.*

Mesh the model with an element size of 2mm, run the solution and display a **Heat Flux** result (Figure 3-4).

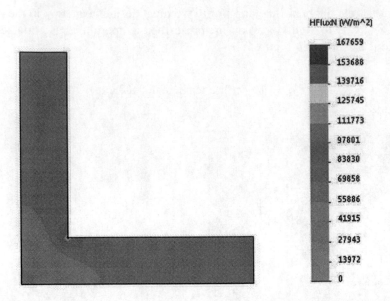

Figure 3-4: Heat flux results obtained with 2mm element size show the maximum heat flux 168kW/m$^2$.

*Review this plot using vector display.*

Notice that the location of the maximum heat flux coincides with the sharp corner.

Copy study *01 sharp* into study *02 sharp*; add a mesh control to the corner (Figure 3-5):

Element size

Transition ratio

Figure 3-5: Mesh control in the sharp corner in study *02 sharp*.

*Use an element size of 0.6mm, and a transition ratio of 1.1 to ensure a smooth transition from dense elements in the corner to coarse elements (2mm) everywhere else in the model.*

Run the analysis then repeat it using progressively smaller elements in the corner; study *03 sharp*: 0.4mm, study *04 sharp:* 0.2mm and study *05 sharp*: 0.1mm. Collect heat flux results in the corner (this will also be the maximum heat flux) from all studies and present them in a graph showing the maximum heat flux as a function of 1/h where h is the element size in the corner (Figure 3-6).

Figure 3-6: Maximum heat flux as a function of the inverse of the element size, h.

*Five points are connected by line only to visually enhance the graph.*

The summary of results presented in Figure 3-6 demonstrates divergence of heat flux results in the presence of a sharp corner. This is in direct analogy to stress divergence in sharp corners in 2D models or sharp edges in 3D models.

Divergence of heat flux results will be further discussed using the HEATING DUCTS model in chapters 5 and 6.

# 4: Thermal analysis of a round bar

## Topics covered

- ❑ Heat transfer by conduction
- ❑ Thermal conductivity
- ❑ Heat transfer by convection
- ❑ Convection boundary conditions
- ❑ Thermal resistance
- ❑ Prescribed temperature boundary conditions
- ❑ Heat power
- ❑ Heat flux

## Project description

A round steel rod is represented by STEEL ROD part model; it has one end in boiling water at 100°C and the other end in melting ice (0°C). The cylindrical face is insulated; no heat is exchanged through that face (Figure 4-1).

Face at 0°C

This face is insulated

Face at 100°C

Figure 4-1: The STEEL ROD model with prescribed temperatures as boundary conditions.

*If no boundary conditions are defined on a face, it means that no heat is exchanged through that face; the face is insulated.*

Our objective is to find the total heat transferred by the rod from the hot to cold side. Notice that conduction is the only heat transfer mechanism present in the model.

Create a thermal study *01 conduction* and define prescribed temperatures as boundary conditions as shown is Figure 4-2.

Figure 4-2: Prescribed temperature defined on the hot side of the rod.

*Define a prescribed temperature of 0°C on the other side.*

Obtain a solution using a default mesh size and review the **Temperature** plot. Follow steps in Figure 4-3 to find the total heat traveling through the rod.

(1)
Right-click
*Results* folder
(2)
Select
List
Heat Power

(3)
Choose Watt,
select
both faces,
click Update

Figure 4-3: Listing Heat Power.

*Heat power in is 8W, heat power out is 8W.*

**Heat Power** window does not have to be called from a result plot. You may right-click results folder and select Heat Power from the pop-up menu.

We use this simple model to compare our heat power result to the analytical solution:

$$Q = \frac{kA(T_{HOT} - T_{COLD})}{L} = \frac{16 \times 0.001 \times (100 - 0)}{0.2} = 8W$$

Where:

$k$ – Thermal conductivity of steel: 16W/m/K

$A$ – Cross section area: 0.001m$^3$

$T_{HOT}$ – Temperature of boiling water: 100°C

$T_{COLD}$ – Temperature of melting ice: 0°C

$L$ – Length of rod: 0.2m

To complete the review of the results of study *01 conduction*, create a **Heat Flux** plot presented as vectors (Figure 4-4).

Figure 4-4: The resultant heat flux presented as vector plot with Vector plot options shown above.

*Heat flux is uniform throughout the model as shown by the numbers at the color legend. The only reason for minute differences is the discretization error introduced by meshing.*

Next we introduce heat transfer through convection. Copy *study 01 conduction* into *02 convection* and delete the prescribed temperature of the cold side. We want to replace this prescribed temperature boundary condition with a convection boundary condition that will give the same temperature distribution along the length of the rod and the same heat flow 8W. What should be the convection coefficient?

First, let's consider what ambient temperature should be defined. We want the cold end of the rod to be at 0°C (273K). If we defined the ambient temperature equal to the previously used prescribed temperature 0°C (273K), then the convection coefficient would have to be infinitely large so the ambient temperature must be lower than 0°C. The lower the ambient temperature, the lower will be the required convection coefficient while 8W of heat power travels through the road. Let's assume the ambient temperature is -10 °C.

Heat transferred by convection is:

$$Q = hA(T_S - T_F)$$

Where:

$Q$ – Heat power (8W) - given

$h$ – Unknown convection coefficient [W/m²/K]

$A$ – Area participating in convective hear transfer (0.001m²) - given

$T_S$ – Temperature of surface (273 K) - given

$T_F$ – Temperature of surrounding fluid (263K) - assumed

From the above equation, the required convection coefficient is:

$$h = \frac{Q}{A(T_S - T_F)} = \frac{8}{0.001 \times 10} = 800 \frac{W}{m^2 K}$$

Using this result, define convection coefficient as shown in Figure 4-5.

Figure 4-5: Convection coefficient on the cold side.

*The convection coefficient replaces the previously used prescribed temperature boundary condition.*

Obtain the solution and find the heat power as shown in Figure 4-6.

Figure 4-6: Heat power in model with prescribed temperature on the hot side and convection on the cold side.

*Compare this with the results shown in Figure 4-3.*

As Figure 4-6 shows, the convection coefficient of 800W/m²/K combined with the temperature gradient between the face and surrounding fluid is equivalent to the prescribed temperature of 273K. From a practical point of view we should notice that the convection coefficient of 800 W/m²/K is quite high; however, it would be possible to get that convection between metal and moving water with melting ice.

Open assembly TWO RODS; the assembly consists of two identical copper rods 100mm long glued with a layer of epoxy resin. The thickness of the glue is 0.5mm: not a very good design but makes for an interesting exercise (Figure 4-7).

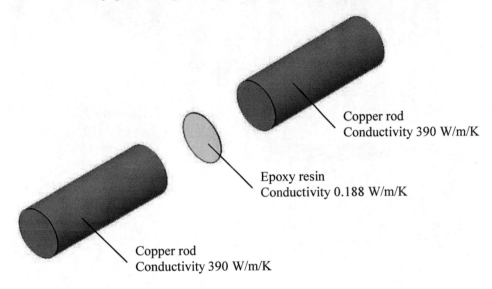

Copper rod
Conductivity 390 W/m/K

Epoxy resin
Conductivity 0.188 W/m/K

Copper rod
Conductivity 390 W/m/K

Figure 4-7: The TWO RODS model features two copper rods glued by epoxy glue.

*The rod material (copper) and glue material (epoxy resin) have vastly different thermal conductivities. Assembly is shown in an exploded view.*

Our objective here is to study the effect of thermal resistance caused by the layer of epoxy. Even though the layer of epoxy is very thin, it has a major effect on heat transfer through the assembly because of its low thermal conductivity. The thinness of the epoxy layer will also cause significant meshing difficulties.

Make sure the assembly is in the *01glue* configuration and create a thermal study called *01 glue*. To ensure a correct aspect ratio of elements meshing the glue layer, apply a **Mesh Control** to the glue component as shown in Figure 4-8.

Select glue from the fly-out menu

Element size 0.5mm

Ratio 1.2

Figure 4-8: Mesh Control applied to glue assembly component.

*A low a/b ratio assures a smooth transition between large elements that mesh the rods, and small elements that mesh the glue. Assembly shown in exploded view.*

The mesh control shown in Figure 4-8 produces one layer of elements in the glue. Second order elements are capable of modeling second order temperature fields and first order (constant) temperature fields. Given that the expected temperature gradient is constant across the epoxy layer, one layer of element will suffice.

Mesh the assembly with the default element size. Apply prescribed temperatures identical to the STEEL ROD exercise: 100°C on one end, 0°C on the other end (Figure 4-9).

Figure 4-9: Prescribed temperature definition at the hot end.

*A prescribed temperature of 0°C on the other end is not shown.*

Run the solution and review the **Temperature** plot. Notice the temperature drop of 8°C over the distance of 100mm in the bar. Compare this to a drop of 84°C over the distance of 0.5mm in glue (Figure 4-10).

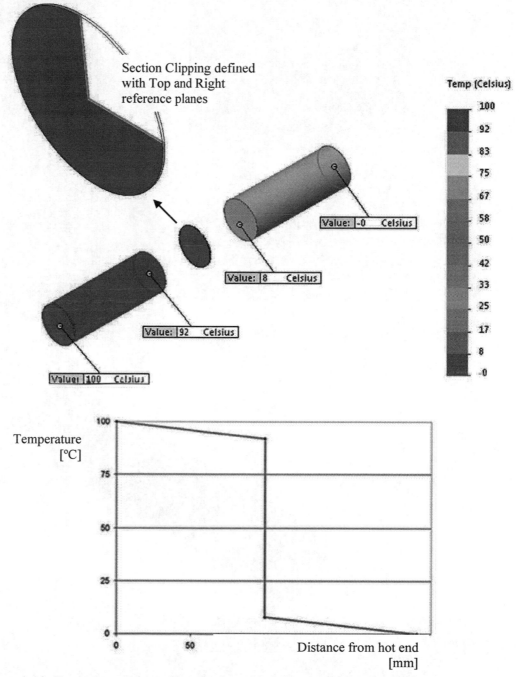

Figure 4-10: Temperature drop along the length of the assembly. Temperature gradient across the thickness of the glue layer may be shown using Section Clipping.

*A rapid temperature drop is caused by a low thermal conductivity of the epoxy glue.*

Total heat flow in the assembly can be displayed as shown in Figure 4-11.

Figure 4-11: Total heat flow through the assembly.

*Since there is no heat loss or gain along the length of the assembly, heat power in equals heat power out 31.5W.*

The thermal resistance of epoxy causes a temperature drop of 83°C over the distance of 0.5mm. Heat flowing through the epoxy is 31.5W. The cross sectional area of the epoxy is 1000mm². Knowing the above we may easily calculate the thermal resistance of the epoxy layer:

$$R = \frac{\Delta T A}{P} = \frac{83 \times 0.001}{31.5} = 0.0026 \frac{Km^2}{W}$$

Where:

$R$ – Distributed (per area) thermal resistance Km²/W

$\Delta T$ – Temperature drop across the layer 83K

$A$ – Cross sectional area: 0.001m³

$P$ – Heat flow (heat power) through the layer

The glue part of the assembly is very small in comparison to the rods, yet it causes a major obstacle in heat flow because of its poor heat conductivity. It also poses major modeling difficulties; we had to apply a mesh control that increased the number of elements in the model very significantly.

The objective of this exercise is to introduce the concept of the layer of thermal resistance. We saw that explicit modeling of the layer of thermal resistance is difficult and gets even more so when the layer gets very thin. Fortunately, there is a better way of modeling the layer of thermal resistance.

Stay with the TWO RODS assembly but switch to the *02 no glue* configuration. The assembly now consists of two parts only. Create a thermal study *02 thermal resistance*. The layer of thermal resistance will be modeled as a **Contact Condition**. Follow Figure 4-12 to define a **Thermal Resistance Contact Condition**.

Figure 4-12: Definition of a Thermal Resistance Contact Condition.

*Use exploded view.*

The value of thermal resistance, 0.0026 Km$^2$/W, comes from a calculation based on the results of the previous study where the layer of thermal resistance was modeled explicitly.

Mesh the assembly with the default element size; no mesh control is needed. Obtain a solution and review the **Temperature** plot.

Figure 4-13: Temperature results in the model with a layer of thermal resistance.

*The temperature drop across the layer of thermal resistance is 83°C.*

The results of study *01 glue* (Figure 4-10) and study *02 thermal resistance* (Figure 4-13) are practically the same. The layer of epoxy glue produces the same temperature drop when modeled either explicitly or as a layer of thermal resistance.

The use of **Thermal resistance Contact Conditions** allows for a very significant simplification of the model, and a faster solution time compared to explicit modeling, as long as the value of thermal resistance in known. If it is not known, it can be found using simple models such as TWO RODS in the *01 glue* configuration. The analysis of real design problems can then be done using **Thermal Resistance**.

*Notes:*

# 5: Floor heating duct – part 1

## Topics covered

- ❑ Heat transfer by conduction
- ❑ Prescribed temperature boundary conditions
- ❑ Heat power
- ❑ Heat flux
- ❑ Heat flux singularities
- ❑ Analogies between structural and thermal analysis

## Project description

A ceramic floor panel used to heat the room is modeled in assembly HEATING DUCTS (Figure 5-1). Hot air flows in the ducts transferring heat to the panel. Heat is dissipated by the panel's top faces. We assume that the side and bottom faces are insulated, therefore no thermal boundary conditions are defined there: no prescribed temperatures, no convection coefficients and no radiation coefficients.

All top faces at 30°C

All inside faces at 80°C

Figure 5-1: HEATING DUCTS assembly model of a ceramic floor panel.

*The assembly consists of five identical parts. The model is shown in 01 CAD configuration.*

Notice that the temperatures shown in Figure 5-1 are prescribed temperatures which are thermal boundary conditions; we will investigate heat flow induced by these boundary conditions. Side faces and bottom faces don't have any prescribed temperature defined but that does not mean that they won't have any temperature. Temperature there will establish itself as a result of heat flow induced by prescribed temperatures shown in Figure 5-1.

We will perform a thermal analysis of this floor panel to find out how much heat is transferred to the room. Because of repeatable geometry and no thermal boundary conditions on either side, the model can be simplified to just one segment. Also, because there is no temperature gradient along the length of ducts (uniform prescribed temperature is defined) the analysis can be further simplified by using a 2D model. A 2D model will also make it easy to demonstrate the heat flux singularity in the presence of sharp edges.

Switch to the *02 Analysis Part1* configuration to review the model (Figure 5-2).

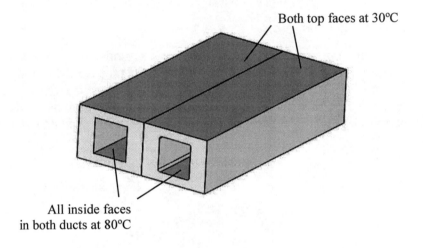

Figure 5-2: HEATING DUCTS assembly in *02 FEA* configuration.

*Notice round edges in the duct on the right.*

Why do we use two segments for analysis even though only one segment could be used? We do that to study the effect of sharp re-entrant edges on heat flux; notice that the left segment has sharp edges; the right one has rounded edges.

The analyzed segment consisting of two ducts is part of a larger assembly. No heat flows through the side faces; therefore, no boundary conditions are defined there. The side faces are treated as if they were insulated.

## *Procedure*

Make sure the model is in configuration *02 Analysis Part 1* and define a thermal study *01 2D* using **2D Simplification**. Follow the steps shown in Figure 5-3.

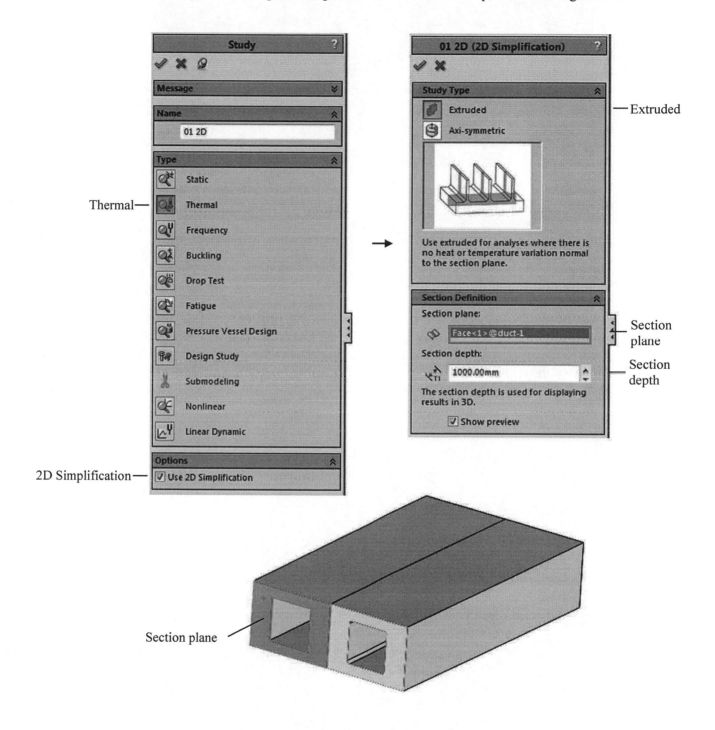

Figure 5-3: Thermal study definition using 2D Simplification.

*Section depth is equal to the length of floor panel 1000mm; this can be measured in the CAD assembly model.*

Geometry ready to be meshed with 2D elements is shown in Figure 5-4.

Figure 5-4: 2D geometry ready to be meshed with 2D elements.

*The left segment has sharp re-entrant corners; the right segment has rounded corners.*

Follow the steps in Figure 5-5 to define prescribed temperatures on the inside edges of the 2D model and Figure 5-6 to define prescribed temperatures on the outside edges of the 2D model. Notice that contact conditions remain as default **Bonded** meaning that there is no layer of thermal resistance between two segments. No action is required on contact conditions.

Figure 5-5: Definition of prescribed temperature on the inside edges.

*A prescribed temperature of 80°C is applied to twelve inside edges: four edges in the left segment and eight edges in the right segment. Prescribed temperature symbols have been made smaller.*

Figure 5-6: Definition of prescribed temperature on the outside edges.

*A prescribed temperature of 30°C is applied to the two outside edges.*

*Symbols of previously defined prescribed temperatures are not shown here for clarity of this illustration.*

Having defined prescribed temperatures on the inside and outside edges we have established a mechanism of heat transfer. Now, mesh the model with a default element size to create a mesh as shown in Figure 5-7.

Figure 5-7: Model meshed with default element size.

*Notice the high turn angle in elements meshing round corners.*

Obtain a solution noticing almost instantaneous results; 2D thermal models solve very fast because of a low number of elements due to the 2D formulation and to the fact that there is only one degree of freedom (temperature) per node. Review temperature result as shown in Figure 5-8.

Figure 5-8: Temperature results from study *2D thermal 01.*

*Temperature is a scalar value; temperature results can only be presented as a fringe plot.*

As Figure 5-8 illustrates, there is little difference between sharp and round corners. The temperature on the inside edges is equal to 80°C; the temperature on the outside edges is equal to 30°C. Everywhere else, a steady state temperature establishes itself as a result of heat flow from hot (80°C) to cold (30°C) edges. Now, create Heat Flux plot as shown in Figure 5-9.

Figure 5-9: Heat Flux results from study *2D thermal 01*. The probed result in the sharp corner is 2733W/m²; the probed result in the round corner is 2776W/m².

*The fringe plot is used to present Heat Flux results. Results in round corners are probed where the horizontal straight line meets the arc.*

Figure 5-9 shows next to no difference in **Heat Flux** between the sharp and round corners, but this will change once we use a more refined mesh.

**Heat Flux** is a vector value; fringe plots show the magnitude but not the direction. To see the direction of heat flow, create a vector plot of **Heat Flux** as shown in Figure 5-10.

Figure 5-10: Heat Flux results from study *2D thermal 01*.

*The vector plot may be modified using Vector plot options shown on the left. Color information is suppressed. Experiment with different Vector plot options.*

Figure 5-10 makes it clear that heat enters and escapes the model only through the edges where prescribed temperatures have been defined. No heat enters or escapes the model through the bottom or sides. No heat is exchanged between the two segments.

Copy study *01 2D* into *02 2D* and add mesh controls as shown in Figure 5-11.

Figure 5-11: Mesh controls and mesh in study *2D thermal 02.*

*An element size of 2mm is defined on all inside edges. A transition of 1.2 creates a large transition zone.*

*Also shown is the mesh created using these controls.*

Using a small element size as shown in Figure 5-11 will demonstrate a very important difference between heat flow in the presence of a sharp and round corner. Obtain the solution of *02 2D* and review the **Temperature** and **Heat Flux** results shown in Figure 5-12 and Figure 5-13.

Figure 5-12: Temperature results from study *2D thermal 02*.

*These results are indistinguishable from the results of study 2D thermal 01.*

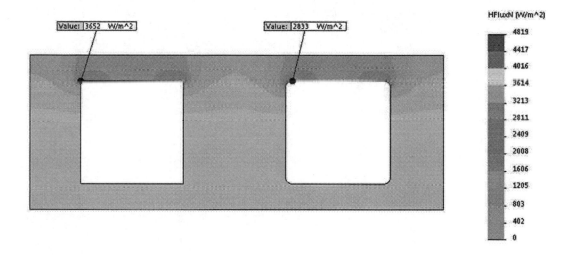

Figure 5-13: Heat Flux results from study *2D thermal 02*. A probed result in the sharp corner shows $4588W/m^2$; a probed result in the round corner shows $2833W/m^2$.

*There is a distinct Heat Flux concentration in sharp corners.*

The small elements used in study *02 2D* reveal a heat flux concentration in the sharp corners. The concentration was previously masked by large elements. To investigate this concentration, we will run three more studies with progressively more aggressive mesh biases as shown in Figure 5-14.

*02 2D*          *03 2D*          *04 2D*          *05 2D*

Figure 5-14: Mesh control in studies *02 2D* through *05 2D*.

*There is no Mesh Control in study 01 2D. The global element size (12mm) is the same in all studies.*

The summary of all results is shown in Figure 5-15.

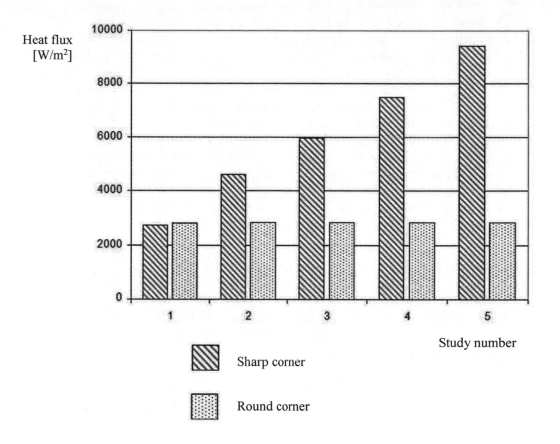

Figure 5-15: Summary of Heat Flux results in five studies.

*The Heat Flux magnitude diverges with mesh refinement in the sharp corner while mesh refinement has no effect on Heat Flux in the round corner.*

Divergent heat flux results in a sharp corner are caused by a singularity. The mathematical model has no heat flux solution in a sharp corner; a mathematician would say that the solution is singular there; an engineer would say that heat flux is infinite in a sharp re-entrant corner. Meshing introduces a discretization error which masks the singularity and may give an appearance of correct results, especially when large elements are used as in study *01 2D*. Mesh refinement reveals the singularity demonstrating divergent results (Figure 5-15). Numerical values of heat flux in sharp and round corners seen in study *01 2D* are close by coincidence. We can't say which study provides "the best" heat flux results in sharp corners because all these results are meaningless. Heat flux results in locations coinciding with sharp corners (or edges in case of 3D models) are entirely dependent on the choice of discretization, and by manipulating the mesh size we can produce as high a result as we want!

Notice that sharp corners have no effect on temperature results. Sharp re-entrant corners (in 2D models) or sharp re-entrant edges (in 3D models) may be acceptable if the data of interest is temperature. They can be also acceptable if heat flux results are sought away from the singularity. However, if the maximum heat flux is the data of interest, rounds must be modeled no matter how small they are. Notice that a sharp (zero-radius) corner or edge is a mathematical abstract, in reality a round is always present even though it may be very small.

To demonstrate the divergence of heat flux results (singularity) we had to use very small elements. It was possible to execute a number of studies in a short time because we used a 2D model. Divergent heat flux can also be demonstrated with a 3D model but at a higher computational effort.

We'll now look at the heat power of the floor panel. Heat power is not sensitive to mesh refinement or heat flux singularities so we may use any of the five studies created so far. Heat power is analogous to the reaction force in a structural analysis.

To list heat power for two segments we use results from study *01 2D* and follow the steps shown in Figure 5-16.

Figure 5-16: The heat power of the segment with sharp corners is 464W, and 456W for the segment with round corners. The total heat power of the two segments is 920W.

*The difference in heat power is due to the different amount of conducting material, not the heat flux singularity.*

To wrap up the analysis of the floor panel with prescribed temperatures for boundary conditions we'll create one more study: *06 3D* where a 3D model will be analyzed to find the total heat power.

Use a standard mesh with element size 20mm to create mesh as shown in Figure 5-17.

Figure 5-17:  Solid element mesh of the 3D model with two segments.

*The elements in the rounds have poor turn angles. It's acceptable for the analysis of heat power on the outside of the model but would require intervention if heat flux results on the inside faces were of interest.*

Heat Power results are shown in Figure 5-18.

Figure 5-18:  The heat power of the segment with sharp corners is 474W, and 448W for the segment with round corners. The total heat power of the two segments is 922W.

*A small difference of results between the 2D model (Figure 5-16) and the 3D model (Figure 5-18) is caused by discretization error which differs between 2D and 3D models.*

*Notes:*

# 6: Floor heating duct – part 2

## *Topics covered*

- ❑ Heat transfer by convection
- ❑ Free and forced convection
- ❑ Convection coefficient
- ❑ Ambient (bulk) temperature

## *Project description*

We have completed part 1 of the floor heat panel analysis modeling heat flow induced by prescribed temperatures: 80°C on the hot side and 30°C on the cold side. Now, we'll take this analysis one step further.

Assume that we have taken the following temperature measurements: air inside: 85 °C, inside faces: 80°C, air outside: 17°C, outside face: 30°C. Notice that the face temperatures are the prescribed temperatures from part 1 of this analysis.

Given the above temperature information we want to find out what convection conditions must be present on the hot and on the cold side to keep these steady state temperatures. For that we use the same assembly model HEATING DUCTS and switch to configuration *03 Analysis Part2*; this configuration has only one segment (Figure 6-1).

Air outside 17°C (290K)
Outside edge 30°C (303K)

Air inside: 85°C (358K)
Inside edges: 80°C (353K)

Figure 6-1: HEATING DUCTS assembly model in *03 Analysis Part3* configuration.

*A 2D Simplification of a segment with round corners is used.*

The bottom outside face is assumed to be insulated, and side faces don't exchange heat because this segment is a part of larger assembly; therefore, no thermal boundary conditions are defined on these faces. We'll proceed in two steps using the 2D model; refer to Figure 6-1 for the location of inside and outside edges.

Step 1 (study *07 2D*):

Thermal boundary conditions on the inside edges are prescribed temperatures of 80°C; this is unchanged from part 1. The convection coefficient on the outside edge will be changed in steps from $10W/m^2/K$ to $1000W/m^2/K$ to determine at what value an average outside edge temperature of 30°C is produced.

Step 2 (study *08 2D*):

The convection condition on the outside edge will be the one found in step 1. The convection coefficient on the inside edges will change in steps from $10W/m^2/K$ to $1000W/m^2/K$ to determine at what value an average inside edge temperature of 80°C is produced.

Once the convection coefficients on both sides have been found, there won't be a need to define prescribed temperatures, and heat flow will be modeled more realistically.

To prepare study *07 2D,* use **2D simplification**. Define **Convection** as shown in Figure 6-2. Define a prescribed **Temperature** of 80°C on the inside edges as in part 1 of this exercise.

Figure 6-2: Convection coefficient on the outside edge.

*A sample value of $100W/m^2/K$ is shown.*

Using default element size run study *07 2D* for the following values of convection coefficients on the outside edge: 10, 50, 100, 200, 300, 500, and 1000. For each value, find the average temperature on the outside edge as shown in Figure 6-3.

Figure 6-3: Average temperature on the outside edge.

*With a convection coefficient of 100W/m²/K, the average temperature of the outside edge is 31.3°C.*

The summary of all runs for convection coefficients on the outside edge of 10, 50, 100, 200, 300, 500, and 1000 is shown in Figure 6-4.

Figure 6-4: Average temperature on the top outside edge as a function of convection coefficient.

*A convection coefficient of $100W/m^2/K$ in combination with an ambient temperature of 290K results in an average temperature of the outside edge of approximately 30°C. Compare this with Figure 6-3.*

Having found the convection coefficient on the outside edge we proceed to finding convection coefficient on the inside edges. Copy study *07 2D* into *08 2D* and delete the prescribed temperature on the inside edges. Make sure that the **Convection** on the outside edge is characterized by a convection coefficient of $100W/m^2/K$ and an ambient temperature of 290K and keep it unchanged throughout the analysis.

Run study *08 2D* for the following values of convection coefficients on the inside edges: 10, 50, 100, 200, 300, 500, and 1000; refer to Figure 6-5.

Figure 6-5: Convection coefficient on the inside edges.

*Sample value of 500W/m²/K is shown.*

For each value of convection coefficient find the average temperature on the inside edge as shown in Figure 6-6.

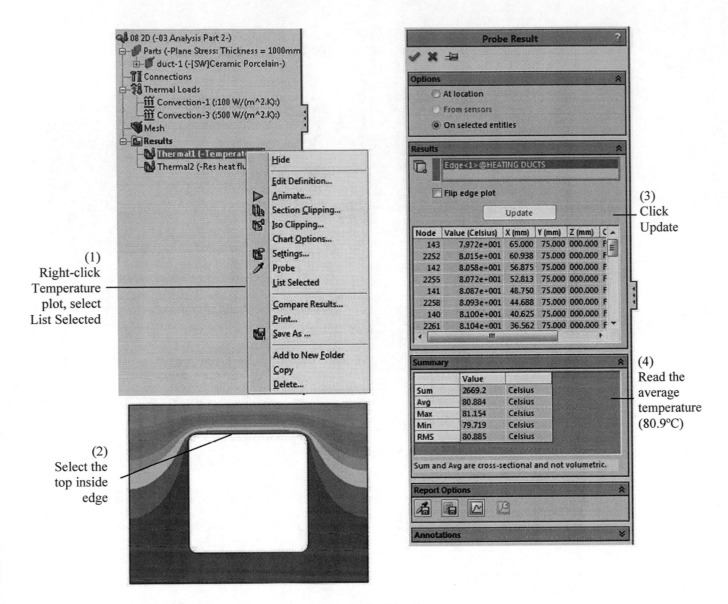

(1)
Right-click
Temperature
plot, select
List Selected

(2)
Select the
top inside
edge

(3)
Click
Update

(4)
Read the
average
temperature
(80.9°C)

Figure 6-6: Average temperature on the inside edge.

*A convection coefficient of 500W/m²/K gives the average temperature of 80.9°C
on the inside edge.*

A summary of all runs for convection coefficients on the inside edges of 10, 50,
100, 200, 300, 500, and 1000 is shown in Figure 6-7.

Figure 6-7: Average temperature on the top inside edge as a function of convection coefficient.

*A convection coefficient of 400W/m²/K gives an average temperature close to 80°C on the inside edge. Compare this with Figure 6-6 showing results for 500W/m²/K.*

Run study *08_2D* one more time with a convection coefficient of 400W/m²/K on the top outside edge and see that the average temperature is 31.4 °C.

In summary, we have found the convection boundary conditions that approximate the prescribed temperature boundary conditions used in part 1 of the HEATING PANEL analysis:

Convection boundary condition on hot side (inside):

Convection coefficient: 400W/m²/K; ambient temp. 85°C (358K);

This boundary condition produces an average temperature 80°C on the top inside edge.

Convection boundary condition on cold side (outside):

Convection coefficient: 100W/m²/K; ambient temp. 17°C (290K);

This boundary condition produces an average temperature 31.4 °C on the top outside edge.

The important difference is that in part 1, the prescribed temperature along the edges is uniform. Using convection boundary conditions, temperature along the edges is no longer uniform, which is more realistic.

Heat Power in the presence of convection boundary conditions is shown in (Figure 6-8).

Figure 6-8: Heat power of one segment.

*Each segment produces 439W heat power.*

Compare this result to the result from part 1 presented in chapter 5.

# 7: Hot plate

## Topics covered

- ❑ Transient thermal analysis
- ❑ Conductive heat transfer
- ❑ Convective heat transfer
- ❑ Heat power
- ❑ Thermostat
- ❑ Thermal inertia

## Project description

A ceramic housing has an embedded heating element producing 1000W of thermal power. The power can be cycled on and off by a thermostat so the plate keeps the surface temperature at about 100°C. We will study temperature fluctuations with time for given thermostat settings.

## Procedure

Open assembly model HOT PLATE, and make sure the assembly is in the *01 heating plate* configuration (Figure 7-1).

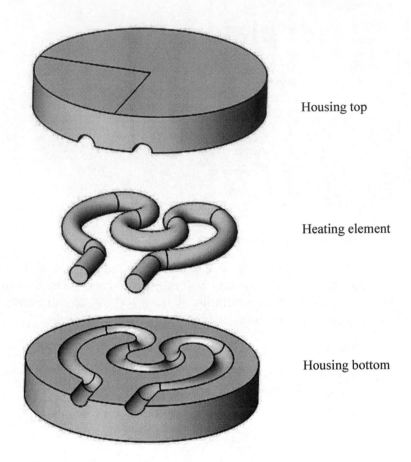

Housing top

Heating element

Housing bottom

Figure 7-1: HOT PLATE assembly in *01 heating plate* configuration.

*The heating plate consists of two identical halves that house a heating element. The exploded view shows all three assembly components. The split line in the housing will be used to define a thermostat position.*

Analysis of temperature fluctuations, while power is cycled on and off, requires transient thermal analysis. Create a Thermal study *01 transient* and set the study properties as shown in Figure 7-2.

Transient analysis —

Total time 2000s —

Time step 60s —

Figure 7-2: Properties of the transient thermal study.

*The duration of analysis and time step usually requires some experimenting during trial runs.*

Using the transient study settings shown in Figure 7-2, the analysis duration will be 2000s; it will be completed in 40 steps, 50 seconds each.

Define **Heat Power** and a **Thermostat** as shown in Figure 7-3.

Figure 7-3: Definition of Heat Power controlled by a Thermostat.

*Select the heating element from the fly-out menu. Place the thermostat in the corner of the split line. The temperature in the location of the thermostat is the temperature that will control the power element on and off.*

With the **Thermostat** setting set up as in Figure 7-3, power is turned on at time t = 0 and it stays on until the temperature reaches 110°C. At 110°C power is turned off until the temperature drops down to 90°C. Then the power is turned on again. It is important to notice that this is the temperature on the outside of the heating plate, not the temperature of the heating element.

Define **Convection** as shown in Figure 7-4. Select all external faces of the ceramic housing. Do not select any face of the heating element.

Figure 7-4: Definition of Convection.

*The faces of the heating elements that stick out of the housing are insulated; do not define Convection conditions for these faces.*

Define an **Initial temperature** to all assembly components as shown in Figure 7-5.

Figure 7-5: Definition of Initial temperature.

*Select all three assembly components from the fly-out menu. Alternatively you may select the assembly.*

Notice that **Initial temperature** must be defined in **Transient** thermal analysis but not in **Steady State** thermal analysis.

Mesh the assembly model with a **Curvature based mesh** using settings shown in Figure 7-6.

<u>Figure 7-6: Curvature based mesh shown in exploded view.</u>

*The maximum element size is 6mm. A minimum of 16 elements in a circle gives an element turn angle of 22.5°.*

A **Curvature based mesh** is more convenient to use because of the many curved faces present in the model. Review the mesh using exploded view to see how the heating element has been meshed. The mesh deficiencies would be easy to miss without the use of exploded view.

We assume an ideal bond between the heating element and ceramic plate; therefore, no thermal resistance is defined there.

The solution of study *01transient* completes in 50 time steps. If you want to reduce the solution time, use a less demanding mesh setting and/or switch to **Standard mesh**. You may also reduce the time of analysis. Once a solution completes, show the **Temperature** plot and follow the steps in Figure 7-7 to create a **Temperature Time History** graph.

**Figure 7-7: Temperature at the Thermostat location during 2000s after power has first been turned on.**

*After the initial warm-up period, the temperature fluctuates between 85C° and 145°C. The temperature time history graph has been formatted in Excel.*

Notice that the range of temperature fluctuation of 85C° to 145°C is wider than what we have defined for our Thermostat. This is due to the effect of thermal inertia; after power has been turned off, the temperature in the thermostat location keeps on climbing for a while. After power has been turned on, the temperature keeps on dropping for a while.

A review of the results for the last performed time step 50 using exploded view is shown in Figure 7-8.

Figure 7-8: Temperature at the end of analysis, time step 50.

*Notice the non-uniform temperature of the heating element.*

Repeat the analysis with different **Heat Power** and **Thermostat** settings to see the effects of different settings on the temperature time history.

Due to mirror symmetry of the HOT PLATE assembly in configuration *01 heating plate* we could have conducted the same analysis on one half of the assembly model. We will take this approach in the continuation of this exercise, where we analyze the heating plate complete with a coffee pot.

Change configuration to *02 coffee pot* and notice that the assembly now includes the hot plate and a glass bowl filled with water. This assembly has mirror symmetry. An assembly cut reduces the model to one half (Figure 7-9).

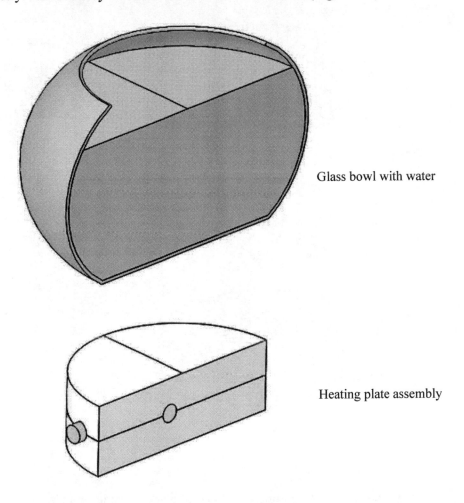

Glass bowl with water

Heating plate assembly

Figure 7-9:  HOT PLATE assembly in *01 coffee* configuration.

*The model is shown in a partially exploded view.*

Our objective is to find the steady state temperature of water when the glass bowl sits on top of the heating plate powered by a constant 200W.  Create study *02 steady state*.

The most important part of this exercise is the definition of heat conductivity of water. Water has already defined properties in the CAD model (Figure 7-10), but these properties must be modified in **Simulation**. Why?

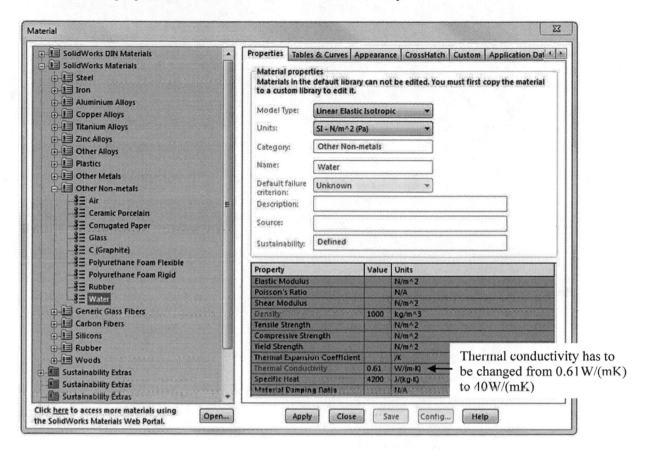

Figure 7-10: Thermal properties of water assigned to CAD model.

*The thermal conductivity must be set to 40W/m/K prior to running analysis. To make this change follow steps in Figure 7-11.*

The thermal conductivity as shown in Figure 7-10 does not take into consideration that water actually mixes while it is being heated and convection, rather than conduction, is mainly responsible for heat transfer in water. Yet, the only mechanism of heat transfer that can be modeled in a solid body (and this is how water is modeled here) is conduction. To account for convection inside the volume of water which we can't model, we have to define an artificially high thermal conduction of 40W/m/K. This value has been found by testing. Modification of thermal conductivity requires definition of custom material. Follow the steps shown in Figure 7-11. Make sure you do the modification in the **Simulation** study, not in the CAD assembly model.

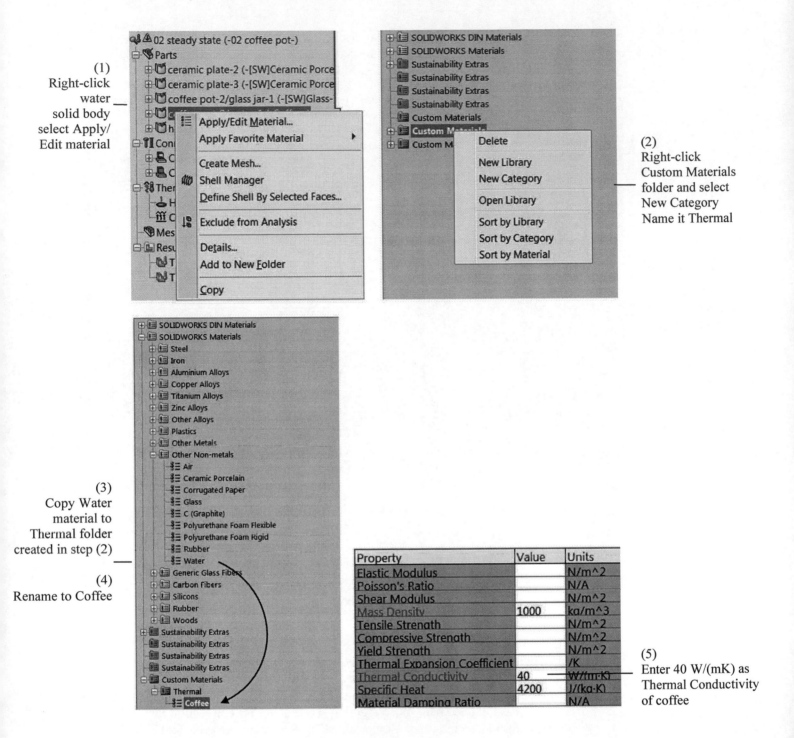

Notice that mass density and specific heat are not required in steady state thermal analysis. We define them to make the model ready for transient thermal analysis should you wish to run it later.

Contact between the heating plate and glass is not perfect and a **Thermal Resistance** contact condition must be defined as shown in Figure 7-12.

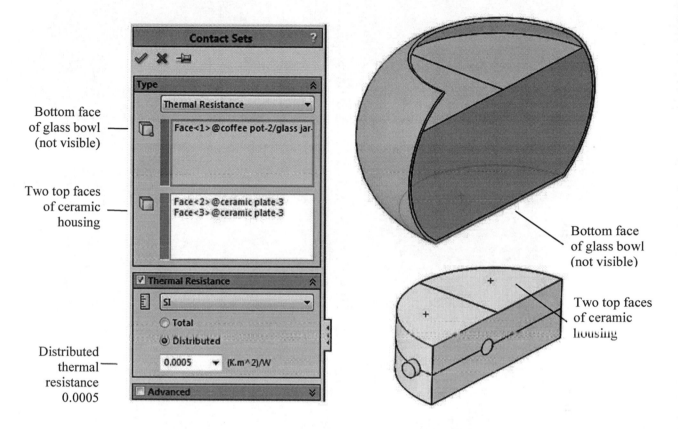

Figure 7-12:  Definition of Thermal Resistance between the heating plate and the glass bowl.

*The value of Thermal Resistance can be determined in testing by measuring the temperature difference between the faces that remain in contact.*

In the steady state analysis we assume that the heating element produces 200W of power. One half of the heating element is modeled, therefore, define 100W. To apply **Heat Power**, refer to Figure 7-3. Since this is a **Steady State** analysis, there is no need to define a **Thermostat**.

Apply **Convection** as shown in Figure 7-13.

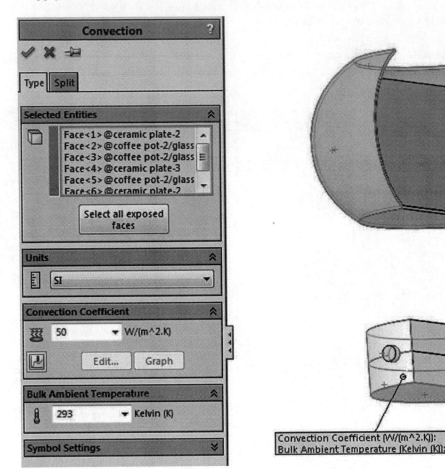

Figure 7-13: Definition of Convection.

*Define a convection boundary condition for all faces exposed to air including water and excluding faces of the heating elements that stick out of the housing. Do not apply convection boundary conditions to any face in the plane of symmetry.*

Due to symmetry, there is no heat flow in the direction normal to the plane of symmetry. The symmetry boundary condition is enforced by not defining convection on the faces in the plane of symmetry.

We have to point out that while defining **Convection** in **SOLIDWORKS Simulation** is easily done, finding the actual value is often the most difficult part of thermal analysis. Applying the same 50W/(m²K) to all faces including water is a modeling simplification which has to be supported by testing.

Having defined **Heat Power** and **Convection**, we have already defined the mechanisms of heat transfer. No Initial **Temperature** is required in **Steady State** thermal analysis. Mesh the model using mesh settings shown in Figure 7-6 and run the solution.

Hide *Water* part in CAD assembly and review the **Temperature** plot as shown in Figure 7-14.

Figure 7-14:  Temperature results; probing shows the effect of the layer of thermal resistance and thermal resistance of glass.

*Notice that the probing location on the side of the hot plate is well defined by the split line, but on the side of the coffee pot you have to "eyeball" probing location. Therefore, your probed result may be slightly different from these shown above.*

*When probing any results, you may deselect Show Node/Element Number and Show X,Y,Z Location for an uncluttered display.*

The thermal resistance illustrated in Figure 7-14 is an inverse of thermal conductivity and has units $K/m^2/W$.

*Notes:*

# 8: Thermal and thermal stress analysis of a coffee mug

## Topics covered

- Transient thermal analysis
- Thermal stress analysis
- Thermal symmetry boundary conditions
- Structural symmetry boundary conditions
- Use of soft springs

## Project description

A ceramic coffee mug at room temperature is filled with boiling water for long enough to reach a steady state temperature, then the water is poured out and the mug is left to cool down. We wish to find thermal stresses in the mug as a function of time during the cooling down process.

## Procedure

Open MUG and review the model (Figure 8-1).

Configuration *01 full*                    Configuration *02 half*

Figure 8-1: Coffee mug in two configurations.

*Split lines on fillets in configuration 02 half are there to define positions of sensors which will be used in this exercise.*

Taking advantage of symmetry we'll use the *02 half* configuration.

First we conduct a **Steady state** thermal analysis to find the initial conditions for the cool down process. Switch to *02 half* configuration and create a **Thermal** study called *01 steady state*. Due to a high convection coefficient between water and porcelain, the inside of the mug will reach almost 100°C, the temperature of boiling water. This can be modeled as a prescribed temperature (Figure 8-2).

Prescribed
temperature —
100°C

Figure 8-2: Prescribed temperature boundary conditions on inside faces of the mug.

*A prescribed temperature is defined for the three inside faces.*

Heat enters the mug through faces where prescribed temperature is defined, travels by conduction through the porcelain, and exits to the surrounding air by convection. Define a convection coefficient on the outside faces including the top face as shown in Figure 8-3.

Convection
Coefficient
50W/m²/K

Bulk
temperature
293K (20°C)

Figure 8-3: Convection boundary conditions on the outside of the mug.

*No convection boundary conditions are defined for the bottom face – it is assumed to be insulated. Also, no convection boundary conditions are applied to the faces in the plane of symmetry.*

By not defining any convection conditions on the faces in the plane of symmetry, we enforce thermal boundary conditions which require that no heat flows in the direction normal to the plane of symmetry.

Before meshing the model we must remember that in the following thermal analysis, we'll conduct the analysis of thermal stresses. In thermal analysis we'll study temperature results which usually does not require "too much" mesh refinement. It is analogous to the analysis of displacements only (and not stresses) in structural analysis. However, in thermal stress analysis, which is structural analysis, we'll study stresses. The mesh must be identical in thermal and thermal stress analyses and therefore, it must satisfy the more demanding requirements of thermal stress analysis. Define mesh controls (as shown in Figure 8-4) on rounds where stress concentrations are expected.

Element size 1mm

Ratio 1.2

**Figure 8-4: Mesh controls on fillets at the base of ear (top illustration) and at the bottom of mug (bottom illustration).**

*1mm element size ensures low turn angle, and a 1.2 transition ratio a/b ensures a smooth transition between locally refined mesh and the rest of the model.*

Use a global element size of 1.8mm to create a mesh with two elements across the wall thickness. Run the solution of study *01 steady state* and review **Temperature** results (Figure 8-5).

Figure 8-5: Steady state temperature results.

*Notice a low temperature gradient across the mug wall. To improve the appearance of this black and white illustration, User defined colors have been used to prepare this plot. This technique is used for many fringe plots presented in this book.*

The temperature results from the steady state thermal analysis conducted in study *01 steady state* are the initial conditions for transient thermal analysis.

Copy study *01 steady state* into *02 transient*. To change from steady state to transient thermal analysis, edit the study properties as shown in Figure 8-6.

Transient analysis —

Total time 600s —

Time step 60s —

Initial temperature —
conditions

Figure 8-6: Properties of *02 transient* study. The definition includes the duration and time step. Initial temperature conditions are taken from the previously completed steady state thermal study *01 steady state.*

*A total time of 600s and a time step of 60s mean that the analysis will be completed in 10 steps.*

Delete the prescribed temperature (water has been poured out) and edit convection conditions to include faces where prescribed temperature was defined before (the inside faces are now exposed to air).

Run the transient solution and display a **Temperature** plot (Figure 8-7).

Figure 8-7: Temperature results from time step 4

*Review other steps to see the change of temperature distribution over time.*

Probe the temperature plot from any time step to produce temperature time history as shown in Figure 8-8.

With temperature results from all 10 steps, we may now find out how thermal stresses change over time. Create a static study *03 stress step 1* and define study properties as shown in Figure 8-9.

Figure 8-9: Properties of static study used for analysis of thermal stresses.

*Select Use soft springs to stabilize the model. The reference temperature at zero strain equals the ambient temperature used in the thermal studies.*

While the thermal boundary condition requires no action (nothing has to be defined on the faces of symmetry), structural boundary conditions must be defined to eliminate out-of-plane motions. Follow Figure 8-10 to define structural symmetry boundary conditions.

Symmetry —

<u>Figure 8-10: Symmetry boundary condition in thermal stress study.</u>

*Symmetry boundary conditions suppress translational degrees of freedom of nodes located on the plane of symmetry in the direction normal to the plane.*

Symmetry boundary conditions will not restrain the model completely. Under the restraints shown in Figure 8-10, the model is able to slide in two directions along the plane of symmetry and to rotate about the axis perpendicular to the plane of symmetry, meaning that the model has 3 rigid body motions (RBM). We could easily add a **Fixed** restraint somewhere to the model but that would change stress results; remember that we want to see thermal stresses which are caused by uneven temperature distribution throughout the model. This is why we use the soft springs option (Figure 8-9) to eliminate these RBMs.

In a thermal stress analysis, nodal temperatures are imported from the thermal to structural (here static) study and that requires that the meshes in the thermal and structural studies are identical. The best way to make sure the meshes are identical is to copy the mesh from study *02 transient* to study *03 stress step 1*.

Run study *03 stress step 1* and display the stress results. Remember that von Mises stress should not be used for evaluating stress results when brittle material (ceramic porcelain) is analyzed; instead, use the maximum principal stress. Refer to chapter 1 of "**Engineering Analysis with SOLIDWORKS Simulation**" for more information. Repeat the process for more time steps to see how stresses change while the mug is cooling down.

P1 stress results from step 1 are shown in Figure 8-11.

Figure 8-11: P1 stress results from step 1.

*Stress concentration locations are indicated by arrows.*

*Display stress results with overlaid mesh to see that the mesh is at best marginal to model highly localized stress concentrations. You may want to repeat this exercise with a more refined mesh.*

Review the stress results from other steps to notice that the highest stress of 41MPa is at the beginning of the cooling process. To calculate the factor of safety, the maximum P1 stress should be compared to the ultimate strength of the ceramic porcelain (173MPa). This comparison gives a factor of safety of 4.2.

To wrap up this exercise, animate displacement results from step 1 to examine the pattern of thermal deformation. Notice that this deformation is caused by thermal effects only. Structural load or restraints have not been used in this analysis.

*Notes:*

# 9: Thermal and thermal buckling analysis of a link

## *Topics covered*

- ❑ Buckling caused by thermal effects
- ❑ Interpretation of Buckling Load Factor

## *Project description*

A rectangular steel bar is supported by hinges on both ends. Its temperature is raised from an initial temperature of 298K to 500K. We want to know if the bar will buckle.

## *Procedure*

Open part model RECT BAR; it consists of one surface (Figure 9-1).

Figure 9-1: Rectangular bar with fixed supports on both ends.

*Fixed supports will be applied on both sides to the round notches.*

To perform a buckling analysis due to thermal effects we need to know the initial temperature (here 298K) and the temperature distribution at the stage where the possibility of buckling is analyzed. We may proceed in two ways. One way would be to run a thermal analysis to find temperatures needed by buckling analysis. However, the temperature will be a uniform 500K and this can be defined directly in the buckling analysis. There is no need for a pre-requisite thermal analysis. If the temperature were distributed non-uniformly, we would have to find it in a prerequisite thermal analysis.

Create a Buckling study called *01b* and verify that the study properties indicate 298K as the reference temperature at zero strain (Figure 9-2). Thermal options default to **Input temperature** so no action is required.

One buckling mode                              Input temperature

Reference temperature at zero strain

Figure 9-2: Properties of buckling study.

*Reference temperature at zero strain is 298K. Selections shown in this illustration are all default.*

Define a **Shell Thickness** 15mm as shown in Figure 9-3.

Figure 9-3: Shell thickness definition.

*Take advantage of Full preview to verify Symmetric placement of shell thickness.*

Define a **Fixed** restraint to both ends (Figure 9-4).

Figure 9-4: Fixed restraints applied to both ends.

*Two Fixed restraints does not allow for rotations.*

Define a **Temperature** of 500K applied to the face as shown in Figure 9-5.

Figure 9-5: Temperature definition.

*Temperature can be defined by selecting the face from either side (top or bottom).*

Run a buckling study using the default element size and display the first buckling mode (Figure 9-6).

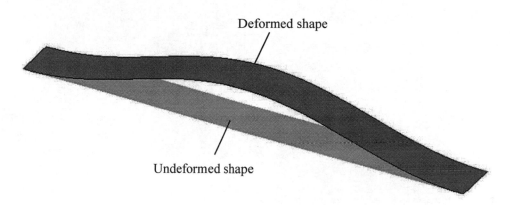

Model name:RECT BAR
Study name:01 b(-Default-)
Plot type: Buckling Amplitude1
Mode Shape : 1  Load Factor = 1.5361
Deformation scale: 84.9061

Deformed shape

Undeformed shape

Figure 9-6: The first buckling shape, buckling load factor 1.54.

*Colors are deselected; undeformed shape is shown.*

The first buckling mode has the shape shown in Figure 9-6 and a buckling load factor (BLF) of 1.54. What does a BLF of 1.54 mean? You'll recall that BLF is a ratio between the load causing buckling and the applied load:

$$BLF = \frac{Buckling\ load}{Applied\ load} = 1.54$$

Notice that the only loads on the model are the hinge reactions caused by the fact that thermal expansion is prevented by immovable hinges. A BLF of 1.54 means that the reaction force in hinge supports would have to increase by a factor of 1.54 in order for buckling to take place. It does not refer directly to temperature.

To find these reactions, we need to run a *Static* study. Create static study *02s*, copy **Shell Definition**, restraints (**Fixed**), loads (**Temperature**), and mesh from the completed buckling study *01b* and obtain a static solution.  Right-click the *Results* folder, select **List result force** and review the reaction forces (Figure 9-7).

Figure 9-7: Reactions at both ends.

*Reactions other than force reaction in X direction are caused by discretization errors.*

The reaction in the X direction is the 368000N compressive load caused by the increase of temperature and restrained thermal expansion. This load would have to increase to 368000N × 1.54 = 566720N in order for buckling to take place.

Euler's formula for beam with both ends fixed gives the buckling load 642252N (dimensions in mm, modulus of elasticity in MPa).

$$F_{buckling} = 4\frac{\pi^2 EI}{l^2} = \frac{4 \times \pi^2 \times 200000 \times 11250}{400^2} = 555165N$$

# 10: Thermal analysis of a heat sink

## *Topics covered*

- ❑ Analysis of an assembly
- ❑ Thermal contact conditions
- ❑ Steady state thermal analysis
- ❑ Transient thermal analysis
- ❑ Thermal resistance layer
- ❑ Thermal symmetry boundary conditions

## *Project description*

We need to find the relationship between the height of cooling fins of an aluminum radiator used to cool an electronic component and the temperature of that component. We will demonstrate that too short of fins does not provide adequate cooling while too long of fins does not offer additional advantages in cooling.

Three configurations of the HEAT SINK TH assembly model are shown in Figure 10-1.

Aluminum radiator

Ceramic microchip

Configuration *01*          Configuration *02*          Configuration *03*

Figure 10-1: Assembly model of a microchip with a radiator.

*HEAT SINK TH assembly consists of two components: a ceramic microchip and an aluminum radiator. All heat generated by the microchip dissipates through the radiator. The two faces of the microchip: the cylindrical side face and the bottom flat face (not visible in this illustration) are insulated. The difference between the three configurations is the height of the cooling fins.*

The double symmetry of the HEAT SINK TH model offers an opportunity to simplify the analysis by using one half or one quarter of the model; here we decide to use half model by working with configurations shown in Figure 10-2.

Configuration *01half*        Configuration *02 half*        Configuration *03 half*

Figure 10-2: *01 half, 02 half* and *03 half* configurations used for analysis.

*We decide not to use one quarter of the model because in this case, double symmetry offers little benefits as compared to one half of the model. We use half of the model to practice thermal symmetry boundary conditions.*

The ceramic microchip generates a heat power of 50W and the aluminum radiator dissipates this heat. The ambient temperature is 27°C (300K). Heat is dissipated to the environment by convection through all exposed faces of the radiator. The microchip is insulated; it cannot dissipate heat directly to ambient air, except through the face touching the radiator. The convection coefficient is 25 W/m²/K in this model; this value corresponds to the natural convection taking place without a cooling fan.

Heat flowing from the microchip to the radiator encounters thermal resistance on the boundary between the microchip and the radiator. Therefore, a thermal resistance layer must be defined on the interface between these two components.

To select the height of the cooling fins, we will determine the temperature and heat flux of the assembly in steady state conditions for the model in three configurations. This will require steady state thermal analysis.

Once we select the height of the cooling fins, we will study the temperature in the assembly as a function of time when the assembly is initially at room temperature and the power is cycled on and off every 10s. This will require transient thermal analysis.

## *Procedure*

Activate configuration *01 half* and create a **Thermal** study called *01 half.* Notice that the *Solids* folder contains two icons corresponding to the two assembly components with material properties already assigned: **Ceramic Porcelain** to the microchip and **1060 Alloy** to the radiator.

Before proceeding, we need to look at the folder called *Connections* which is found in the *01 half* study. By default, the **Global Contact** between parts in an assembly is **Bonded**. As the name implies, all parts in the assembly behave as one and heat encounters no resistance flowing from one part to another. We need to change it by defining a **Contact Set** which overrides the **Global Contact** condition.

Right-click the *Connections* folder and select **Contact Set** to open the **Contact Set** window shown in Figure 10-3. Select **Thermal Resistance** with **Node to surface** as the contact type. This contact condition overrides the global **Bonded** contact condition. Use the exploded view to select the contacting faces and enter a **Distributed Thermal Resistance** of $0.001 Km^2/W$. This value is usually obtained by testing. Notice that the units of thermal resistance are the reciprocal of the units of thermal convection.

Figure 10-3: Definition of Thermal Resistance Contact Set.

*We need to define a local Contact Set for contacting faces in order to introduce a thermal resistance layer between the faces. Use the exploded model view to define the Contact Set. This can only be done as a local Contact Set using the Node to surface option in Advanced options.*

Next, specify the heat power generated in the microchip. To do this, right-click the *Thermal loads* folder to open the pop-up menu. Select **Heat Power…** to open the **Heat Power** window (Figure 10-4), and then from the **SOLIDWORKS** fly-out menu select the *MICROCHIP* assembly component and define a 25W heat power which is one half of the heat power generated in the microchip. This applies heat power to the entire volume of the selected component.

Figure 10-4: Heat Power is applied to the entire volume of the microchip.

*Notice that reversing the direction in the Heat Power definition window would produce cooling.*

So far we have assigned material properties to each component, a heat source, and a thermal resistance layer. In order for heat to flow, we must also establish a mechanism for heat to escape the model. This is accomplished by defining convection coefficients.

Right-click the *Thermal Loads* folder to open a pop-up menu and select **Convection...** to open the **Convection** window (Figure 10-5). Select all faces of the RADIATOR except the one touching the MICROCHIP and the face representing the symmetry plane. Do not select any face of the MICROCHIP. Enter 25 W/m$^2$/K as the value of the convection coefficient for all selected faces and enter the **Bulk Ambient Temperature** as 300K.

Figure 10-5: Definition of convection coefficient on the outside faces of the radiator.

*Use this window to specify both the Convection Coefficient and the Ambient Temperature.*

The last step before solving is creating the mesh. For accurate heat flux results, we need several elements modeling the fillet curvature. This can be done either using a **Standard Mesh** with mesh controls applied to all six fillets or using a **Curvature based mesh** as shown in Figure 10-6. We will use this method.

Global element size 2.5mm

16 elements per circle

<u>Figure 10-6: A curvature based mesh assures correct meshing of fillets without the use of mesh controls. Use 16 elements per circle to ensure a low turn angle.</u>

*Notice that a curvature based mesh produces a low element turn angle at the base of each fin.*

We use a **Curvature based mesh** with settings shown in Figure 10-6 for all **Steady State** studies, even though the heat flux will not be analyzed. The **Transient** analysis will be performed with a default standard mesh.

Once the solution is ready, examine the temperature results. Repeat the analysis for *02 half* and *03 half* configurations. The summary of all temperature results is shown in Figure 10-7.

Configuration *01 half*
Fins 10mm

Configuration *02 half*
Fins 20mm

Configuration *03 half*
Fins 30mm

Figure 10-7: The summary of temperature results of steady state analyses in three configurations.

*Notice that the temperature of the radiator is practically uniform due to high conductivity of aluminum. Temperature in the microchip is the highest at the bottom.*

To decide if the fin height should be increased past 30mm, we present the results in a graph, shown in Figure 10-8.

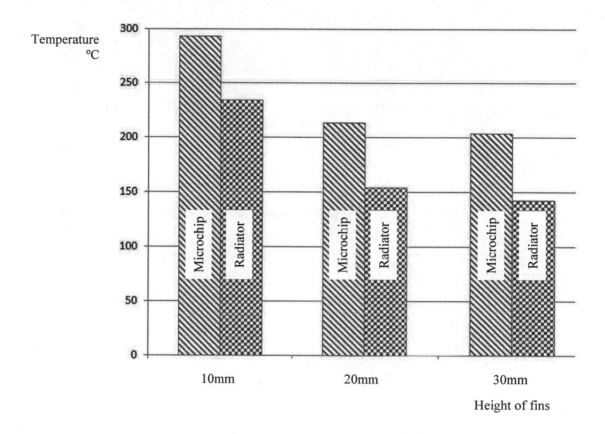

<u>Figure 10-8: The summary of maximum temperature results from the steady state analyses in three configurations.</u>

*Notice that the increase in fin length from 10mm to 20mm has a much stronger effect than the increase from 20mm to 30mm.*

A review of the graph shown in Figure 10-8 proves that increasing the height of fins follows the law of diminishing returns. Here, we decide that 30mm high fins offer sufficient cooling and proceed with a transient analysis of the model in the *03 half* configuration.

Copy the study *03 half* into *03 half transient* and make it into a **Transient** study by defining properties as shown in Figure 10-9.

Figure 10-9: Properties of the transient thermal study.

*Analysis will be conducted for 3000s in 20s intervals.*

Overwrite the mesh copied from study *03 half* by meshing the assembly with a standard mesh using a default global element size to reduce the number of elements. A low number of elements is desired to reduce solution time.

As in any transient thermal analysis, the **Initial temperature** must be defined for all components. Define it as shown in Figure 10-10.

Figure 10-10: Initial temperature defined for both assembly components.

*Select both components from the fly-out menu not shown in this illustration.*

The definition of the convection coefficient remains unchanged, but the heat power definition must be modified to model it as a function of time. Open the Excel file located in the same folder as HEAT SINK TH and follow the steps shown in Figure 10-11.

Figure 10-11: Definition of transient heat power.

*Copy the table from HEAT SINK TH.xlsx. The table is highlighted in yellow in the spreadsheet.*

Run the analysis and display a temperature plot from any time step; it does not have to be the last step. Probe the radiator and create a plot of temperature as a function of time by following the steps shown in Figure 10-12.

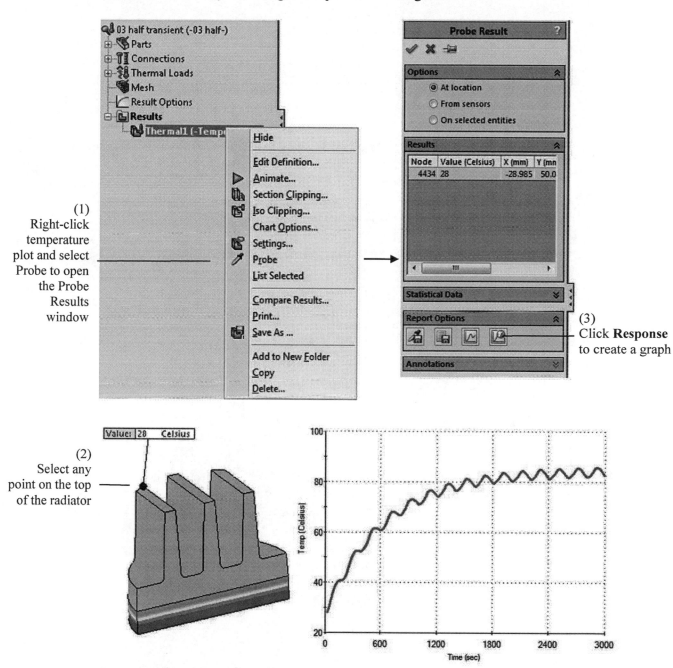

(1)
Right-click temperature plot and select Probe to open the Probe Results window

(3)
Click **Response** to create a graph

(2)
Select any point on the top of the radiator

Figure 10-12: Temperature of radiator as function of time.

*The temperature of radiator is almost uniform; therefore, any point away from the microchip may be selected for probing temperature results.*

The graph in Figure 10-12 shows that after 3000s, the temperature fluctuations stabilize in the range of 82-86°C.

All temperature plots defined so far have shown uniform temperature in the heat sink because the temperature gradient in the heat sink is very low as compared to the temperature gradient in the microchip. To see the temperature gradient in the heat sink, use **Chart Options** to adjust the range of temperature as shown in Figure 10-13.

Figure 10-13: Temperature in radiator in the last performed step at time t=3000s.

*The temperature range shown in the plot is 82.0 – 83.7°C. Microchip component is not shown. Custom colors are used.*

# 11: Radiative power of a black body

## *Topics covered*

- ❑ Heat transfer by radiation
- ❑ Emissivity
- ❑ Black body
- ❑ Radiating heat out to space
- ❑ Transient thermal analysis
- ❑ Heat power
- ❑ Heat energy

## *Project description*

A graphite ball has a surface area of $1m^2$. It is surrounded by a vacuum and its initial temperature is 0K. At time t=0s, a source of power activates such that 1000W is generated uniformly in the ball volume. We want to know the steady state temperature of the ball's surface and time required to reach that steady state, assuming the ball's surface has the emissive properties of a black body.

The objective of this somewhat abstract problem is to study a single body radiating heat out to space without any interference from other objects. This problem has a very simple analytical solution so we'll be able to compare numerical and analytical results.

## *Procedure*

Open GRAPHITE BALL and create a thermal study called *01 transient*. Use the study properties to define a study as transient (Figure 11-1).

Total time

Time increment

<u>Figure 11-1: Properties of transient thermal study.</u>

*Most often some trial runs are required to define a Total time and Time increment.*

As always, in a transient thermal analysis, an initial temperature is required. Follow Figure 11-2 to define it as absolute zero.

Figure 11-2: Definition of initial temperature.

*From the fly-out menu, select the Solid Body to apply the initial temperature to the entire volume (solid body). Since there is only one Solid Body in this model, this applies the initial temperature to the entire model*

Figure 11-2 shows the definition of initial temperature to the entire volume of the model. Notice that if the surface is selected instead of the volume, then that surface is given the temperature; the rest of the model is at a default of 0K. Therefore, in this specific example, it would not make a difference to apply the initial temperature to the face or to the volume.

Define **Radiation** boundary conditions to the surface of the sphere as shown in Figure 11-3.

<u>Figure 11-3: Radiation boundary conditions.</u>

*Radiation boundary conditions are applied to the face, not to the volume.*

An **Emissivity** of 1 means that the ball's face has the emissive properties of a black body. Nothing is better at emitting radiative heat than a black body. A **View Factor** of 1 in combination with a **Surface to ambient** type of radiation boundary condition means that all heat is radiated out to space without interfering with anything.

Define **Heat Power** as shown in Figure 11-4.

<u>Figure 11-4: Definition of heat power.</u>

*From the fly-out menu, select the Solid Body to apply Heat Power to the entire volume of this model.*

Mesh the model with a default mesh and run the solution; notice that the solution is completed in 15 steps. Display the **Temperature** results from the last step using a section plot as shown in Figure 11-5.

Step 15

<u>Figure 11-5: Temperature results from step 15.</u>

*The section plot indicates a very low temperature gradient (0.8K) in the ball cross section. The color legend changes from 364.0K to 364.8K.*

The temperature difference between the core (364.8K) and the outside face (364.0K) indicates that the transient heat transfer is still in process, but for any practical purpose the gradient 0.8K may be ignored and we may consider this to be the steady state.

To graph a temperature time history, probe any location on the face of the ball. Disable section plot prior to probing and follow the steps in Figure 11-6.

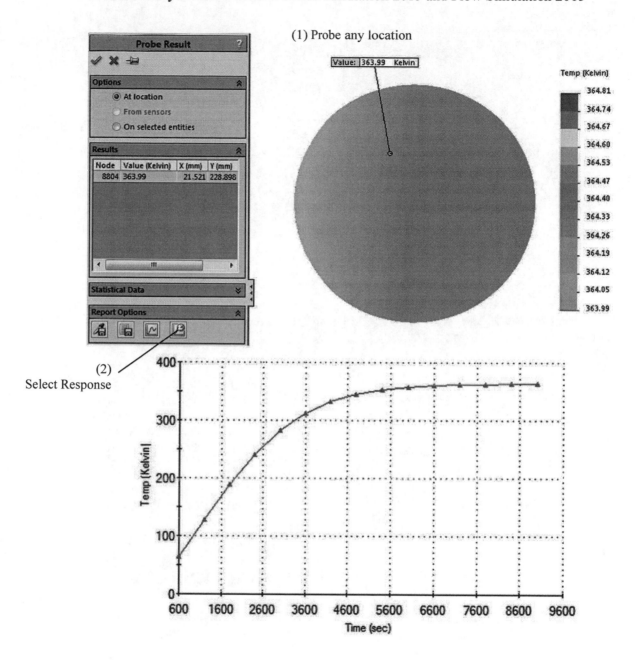

<u>Figure 11-6: The temperature at step 15 (top) and the temperature time history from steps 1-15.</u>

*The ball's face temperature is uniform so you may probe any location.*

As the graph in Figure 11-6 indicates, the steady state temperature has been practically reached after about 7000s. The temperature shown in Figure 11-6 is therefore the steady state temperature that has established itself as a result of radiative heat flow.

Review the **Heat Power** at step 15 and **Heat Energy** produced during the 9000s (Figure 11-7).

Heat Power

Time
9000s

Heat Energy

Time period
from 0 to 9000s

Response graph

Heat Power emitted by the surface
at step 15 (9000s)

Heat Energy that escaped
through ball surface during 9000s

Figure 11-7: Heat Power at step 15 and total Heat Energy during 9000s. Select
the face in both windows.

*After 9000s the face is emitting 995W, the total energy emitted by radiation
during 9000s is 5.325MJ. Review Response Graph in Heat Power window.*

Use windows as shown in Figure 11-8 to collect information about heat power radiated out at the end of each step. The summary is shown in Figure 11-9.

Step 1: 690W          Step 10: 926W          Step 15: 995W

Figure 11-8: Energy radiated out by the ball surface during selected steps.

*Remember to click Update every time the Solution Step is changed. Review response Graph in any of the above windows.*

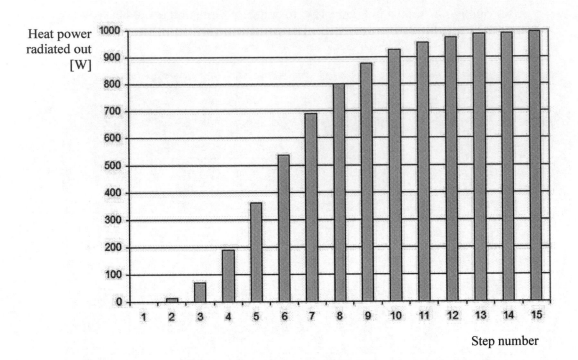

Figure 11-9: Heat power radiated out by the ball surface as function of step number.

*Compare this graph with the temperature time history graph in Figure 11-6.*

The same graph may be created automatically by selecting **Response Graph** in windows shown in Figure 11-7.

This very simple model geometry makes it easy to compare the results of the numerical simulation with analytical results. Review model and results to notice that:

The emissivity of ball face is $\varepsilon = 1$ (it is a black body)

Stefan-Boltzmann constant $\sigma = 5.67 \times 10^{-8}$ W/m²/K⁴ (see chapter 1)

Heat flux $q = 995\text{W}/1\text{m}^2 = 995\text{W/m}^2$ (Figure 11-8)

Using the above, the surface temperature $T_S$ can be found from the Stefan-Boltzman law:

$$q = \varepsilon \sigma T_S^4$$

$$T_S = \left(\frac{q}{\varepsilon \sigma}\right)^{0.25} = \frac{995}{1 \times 5.67 \times 10^{-8}} = 364K$$

This result is the same as the numerical result $T_S = 364K$ shown in Figure 11-5. If results were truly steady state, we could use a heat flux of 1000W/m² from the input data.

We will now review energy balance.

Specific heat of graphite: $c = 44$ J/kg/K (read from material properties)

Mass of graphite ball: 210.64kg (measure this in the SOLIDWORKS model)

Energy used to raise the temperature of the graphite ball from 0K to 364K:

$$E_C = mc\Delta T = 210.64 \times 44 \times 364 = 3374kJ$$

Energy radiated out from the ball's surface (Figure 11-7):

$$E_R = 5325kJ$$

Total energy:

$$E = E_C + E_R = 3374kJ + 5325kJ = 8699kJ$$

This result is within 4% of the total energy calculated as:

$$E = P \times t = 1000W \times 9000s = 9000kJ,$$

where $P$ is heat power and $t$ is the duration of the analyzed process.

*Notes:*

# 12: Radiation of a hemisphere

## *Topics covered*

- ❑ Heat transfer by radiation
- ❑ Emissivity
- ❑ Radiating heat out to space
- ❑ View factors
- ❑ Heat power

## *Project description*

A nickel hemisphere is heated in its volume with 800W. It is insulated on the outside faces while the concave face exchanges heat by radiation with a large enclosure at 30°C. The surface emissivity is 0.4. The hemisphere is in vacuum. We'll calculate the steady state temperature of the hemisphere.

## *Procedure*

Open model HEMISPHERE and create a thermal study called *01 steady state* (Figure 12-1).

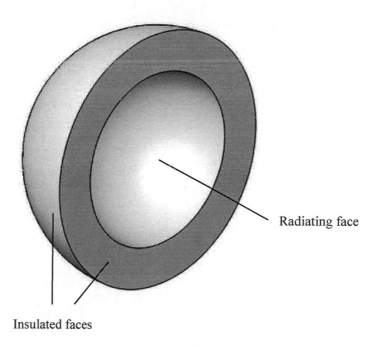

Radiating face

Insulated faces

Figure 12-1: Hemisphere model.

*The concave face radiates heat out to open space characterized by an ambient temperature of 30°C. The other two faces are insulated. Heat transfer takes place only through the concave face.*

Define **Heat Power** as shown in Figure 12-2.

Figure 12-2: Heat Power is generated in the entire volume of the model.

*Select Solid Body Revolve1 from the fly- out menu.*

Define **Radiation** boundary conditions as shown in Figure 12-3.

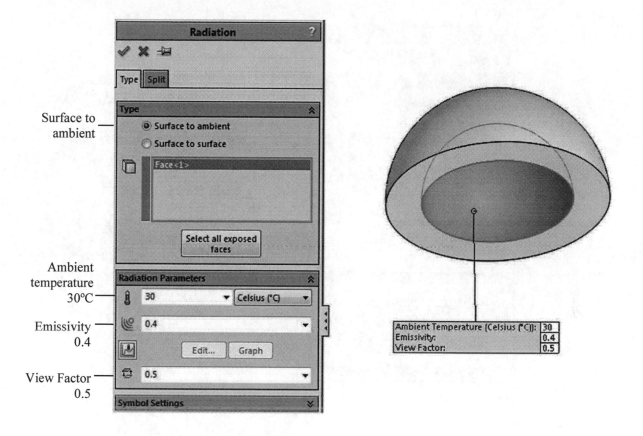

Surface to ambient

Ambient temperature 30°C

Emissivity 0.4

View Factor 0.5

<u>Figure 12-3: Radiation boundary conditions.</u>

*Radiation boundary conditions are defined for the concave face.*

You may conceptualize **Ambient temperature** as the temperature of a large enclosure in which the HEMISPHERE is located: Figure 1-7 (2). **Emissivity** is a measure of how well the face emits radiation in comparison to a black body which has emissivity equal to 1. **View Factor** is a measure of what portion of radiation is radiated out directly to space. If radiation boundary conditions are **Surface to ambient** with a **View Factor** equal to 1, all power is radiated out directly to space as was the case with GRAPHITE BALL in chapter 11. The **View Factor** of 0.5 used in the HEMISPHERE accounts for the fact that this concave face can "see itself"; some heat radiated out hits this surface again before being finally radiated out to space.

Mesh the model using a **Curvature based mesh** (Figure 12-4).

Figure 12-4: Mesh parameters are all on defaults.

*A curvature based mesh is a natural choice for this type of geometry.*

Obtain a solution and show a **Temperature** plot (Figure 12-5).

Figure 12-5: Temperature result plot.

*In radiation problems temperature should be expressed in Kelvins.*

Notice the practically uniform temperature distribution in the model due to the high thermal conductivity of nickel.

Follow steps in Figure 12-6 to review **Heat Power** results and verify that all power generated in the volume to HEMISPHERE is radiated out by the concave face where the radiation boundary conditions have been defined.

Figure 12-6: Heat Power radiated out is 800W.

*The generated heat leaves the HEMISPHERE through the face where the radiation boundary conditions have been defined.*

# 13: Radiation between two bodies

## *Topics covered*

- ❑ Heat transfer by radiation
- ❑ Emissivity
- ❑ Radiating heat out to space
- ❑ View factors
- ❑ Heat power
- ❑ Closed system
- ❑ Open system

## *Project description*

Heat power is generated in the volume of one solid body and is radiated out to the second body which dissipates it by convection. This example may have little relevance to any practical problem but it allows studying different options in radiation heat transfer available in **SOLIDWORKS Simulation**.

## *Procedure*

Open assembly model BLOCKS (Figure 13-1) and create a thermal study *01 surface to surface closed system.*

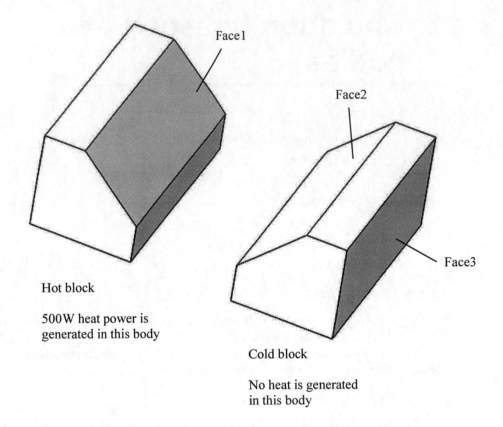

Face1

Face2

Face3

Hot block

500W heat power is
generated in this body

Cold block

No heat is generated
in this body

Figure 13-1: BLOCKS assembly consists of two identical solid bodies.

*There are two mechanisms responsible for heat transfer in this model: radiation and convection. Face 1 and Face 2 exchange heat by radiation. Face 3 dissipates heat by convection.*

In **Simulation**, heat transfer between detached bodies can only be exchanged by radiation. This is because convection models heat exchange between a face and ambient, not between two faces.

Apply **Heat Power** as shown in Figure 13-2.

Figure 13-2: 500W Heat Power is applied to the left block.

*Select the block from the fly-out menu.*

Apply **Radiation** boundary conditions as shown in Figure 13-3.

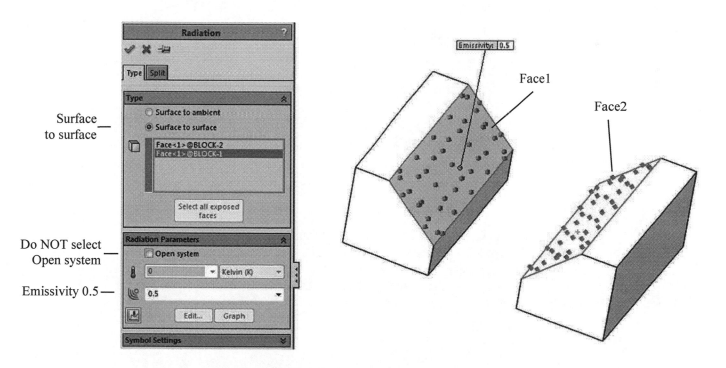

Figure 13-3: Radiation boundary conditions. Heat is exchanged by radiation between the selected Face1 and Face2.

*Radiation symbols are shown in this illustration.*

It is important to comment on the **Radiation** boundary conditions defined in Figure 13-3. Without selecting **Open system** we assume that all heat radiated out of face 1 travels without any loss to face 2. This is of course unrealistic but the objective of this exercise is to demonstrate differences between **Radiation** boundary conditions in Open and Closed systems.

So far we have established a mechanism of heat flow by radiation between two bodies. Now we have to define how heat exits the system. Define **Convection** boundary conditions as shown in Figure 13-4.

Convection
Coefficient
50W/m²/K)

Ambient
temperature
300K

Figure 13-4: Convection boundary conditions; the selected face exchanges heat with fluid.

*Convection symbols are shown in this illustration.*

The face where the **Convection** boundary condition is defined must be in contact with a fluid to be able to exchange heat by convection. The faces with **Radiation** boundary conditions are exposed to a vacuum but no heat is radiated out to space because **Open system** is deselected; all other faces are insulated, meaning that no heat exchange by convection takes place there.

Mesh the model with a default mesh and run the solution. Review the
**Temperature** plot as shown in Figure 13-5.

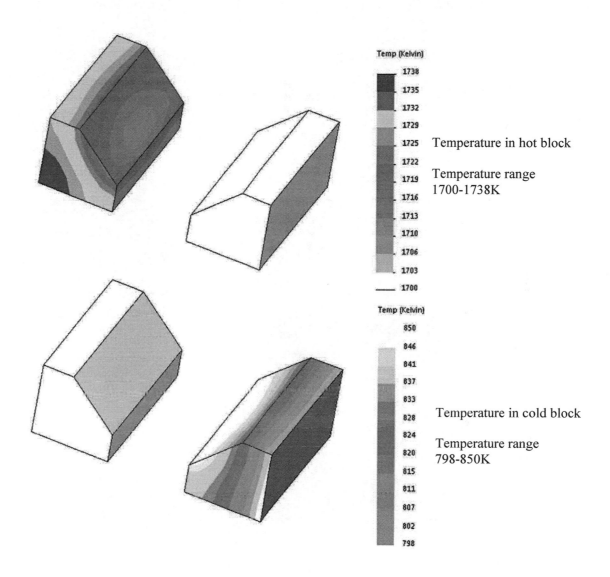

Temperature in hot block

Temperature range
1700-1738K

Temperature in cold block

Temperature range
798-850K

Figure 13-5: Temperature results.

*Two plots with different temperature ranges are used to show temperature
distribution in the hot and cold blocks.*

*User Defined colors have been defined in Chart options.*

Temperature results are presented in Figure 13-5 using two plots with different temperature ranges: 1700-1738K to show temperature distribution in the block radiating out heat and 798-850K to show temperature distributions in the block receiving heat by radiation.

Review **Heat Flux** results using a vector plot as shown in Figure 13-6.

Figure 13-6: Heat Flux results.

*The vector plot offers a convenient way to analyze the path of heat flow. Vector plot options used in this plot are shown.*

To verify that the entire heat generated in the hot block indeed travels through a vacuum to the cold block, we may probe **Heat Power** on any of the three faces that participate in heat exchange as shown in Figure 13-7.

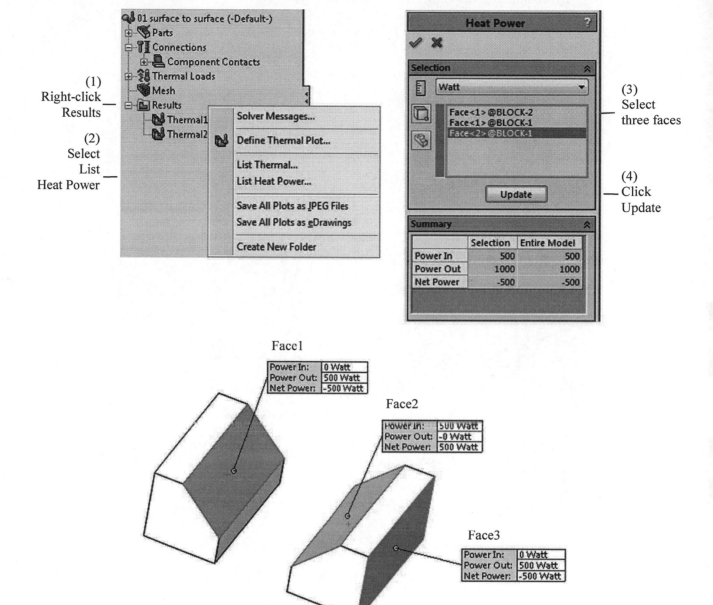

**(1)**
Right-click
Results

**(2)**
Select
List
Heat Power

**(3)**
Select
three faces

**(4)**
Click
Update

Face1

| | |
|---|---|
| Power In: | 0 Watt |
| Power Out: | 500 Watt |
| Net Power: | -500 Watt |

Face2

| | |
|---|---|
| Power In: | 500 Watt |
| Power Out: | -0 Watt |
| Net Power: | 500 Watt |

Face3

| | |
|---|---|
| Power In: | 0 Watt |
| Power Out: | 500 Watt |
| Net Power: | -500 Watt |

Figure 13-7: Heat Power results.

*Heat Power is probed on all faces where thermal boundary conditions have been defined.*

As the sign of **Net Power** indicates, both Face1 and Face3 lose heat while Face2 gains heat. Compare this with Figure 13-6.

This completes the analysis carried under the assumption of a closed system.
Now copy the study *01 surface to surface closed system* into study *02 surface to surface closed system*. The difference between these two studies is that the radiation boundary condition now specifies **Open system** (Figure 13-8).

Closed system   Open system

Ambient temperature

Study *01 surface to surface closed system*     Study *02 surface to surface open system*

Figure 13-8: Radiation boundary conditions in two studies.

*Open system allows the heat to be radiated out to space.*

Notice that while specifying **Open system** we also have to define **Ambient Temperature** because heat is now radiated out to space. **Ambient temperature** is the temperature of a distant enclosure inside in which the two blocks are located as shown in Figure 1-7 (2).

**Temperature** and **Heat Flux** results in **Open system** are shown in Figures 13-9 and 13-10.

Temperature in hot block

Temperature range
1010-1036K

Temperature in cold block

Temperature range
317-319K

Figure 13-9: Temperature results in Open system.

*Two plots with different temperature ranges are used to show temperature distribution in the hot and cold blocks.*

Figure 13-10: Heat Flux results in Open system.

*Heat Flux vectors are barely visible in Cold block because very little heat reaches to the Cold block. Most of it is lost to the surrounding space.*

Follow the same steps as shown in Figure 13-7 to probe **Heat Power** and find out how much heat is transferred from the hot block to the cold block and how much is radiated out to space (Figure 13-11).

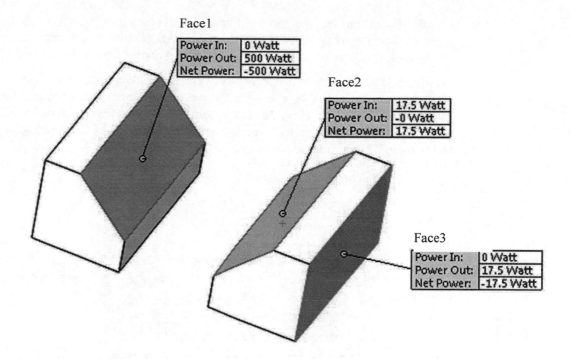

Figure 13-11: Heat Power results in an Open system.

*Out of 500W leaving Face1 only 17.5W reaches Face2.*

As Figure 13-11 shows, 500W - 17.5W = 482.5W is radiated out to space. The 17.5W of heat that reaches the Cold block travels by conduction through the Cold block to the face where the **Convection** boundary condition is defined. Upon reaching it, it is dissipated by convection to the surrounding fluid.

To illustrate an important difference between the study with **Closed system** and **Open system**, delete or suppress the **Convection** boundary condition in study *01 surface to surface closed system* and try running it. This results in an error (Figure 13-12) because in a closed system, in the absence of **Convection**, a mechanism of heat transfer does not exist.

Figure 13-12: An error message is displayed when the solution is attempted with a Closed system and no Convection boundary conditions.

*Direct Sparse solver and FFEPlus iterative solver produce different error messages.*

If you suppress **Convection** using an **Open system**, the solution will be completed. This is because Face1 and Face2 can now exchange heat not only between themselves, but also can radiate it out to space (Figure 13-13).

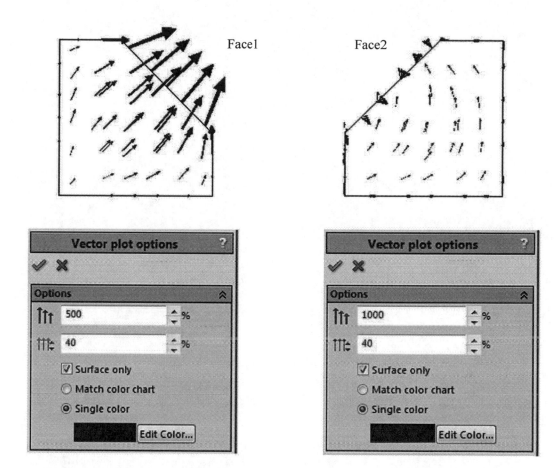

Figure 13-13: In the absence of convection in the Open system, heat enters and exits the Cold block through Face2.

*To improve clarity of Vector plots different Vector options are used for hot block and cold block.*

*Notes:*

# 14: Heat transfer with internal fluid flow

## Topics covered

- ❏ Introduction to Flow Simulation
- ❏ Using Flow Simulation for finding convection coefficients in internal fluid flow
- ❏ Interfacing between Flow Simulation and Thermal analysis
- ❏ Interfacing between Flow Simulation and structural (Static) analysis

## Project description

In the preceding chapters we introduced thermal analysis as a tool of heat transfer analysis in solids. On many occasions we pointed it out that the heat exchange between a solid body and the surrounding fluid is governed by boundary conditions called convection coefficients but the fluid flow itself is not modeled in **SOLIDWORKS Simulation**. To define heat exchange between the face of a solid and the surrounding fluid, we would enter known convection coefficients and a reference (ambient) temperature. These convection coefficients could have come from testing or from the correlation between tests and numerical analyses.

In this chapter we use a very different approach; we'll find the convective boundary conditions (convection coefficients and ambient temperature) by simulating fluid flow. We'll then use those convective boundary conditions to analyze heat transfer in a solid body the way we were doing that in chapters 1-13.

Numerical simulation of fluid flow belongs to a discipline called **Computational Fluid Dynamics (CFD)**. In **SOLIDWORKS** it has been implemented as an add-in called **Flow Simulation** which is different from **SOLIDWORKS Simulation**. Using **Flow Simulation** is a topic for a separate book, we will introduce it here only in a limited scope as required to use the results of **Flow Simulation** in a **Thermal** and **Static** or **Nonlinear** analyses which of course belong to **SOLIDWORKS Simulation**.

We'll be using two add-ins to **SOLIDWORKS**: **SOLIDWORKS Simulation** and **SOLIDWORKS Flow Simulation**. These similar and somewhat confusing names require some introduction. First, let's agree on the following name convention: **Simulation** will mean the add-in in called **SOLIDWORKS Simulation**; this is what we have been using exclusively until now. **Flow Simulation** will mean another add-in used for **CFD**.

**Simulation** is based on a numerical technique called **Finite Element Method** which we customarily call **FEA**. **Simulation** is used for structural and thermal analyses of solid bodies. **Flow Simulation** is based on a numerical technique called **Finite Volumes (FV)**. It is used for the analysis of fluid flow which may (but does not have to) include heat transfer.

If heat transfer is not considered in the analyzed problem, then **Flow Simulation** is concerned only with the space where fluid flow occurs. This may be a cavity inside a solid and/or space around a solid.

If heat transfer is included in the analysis of fluid flow, then **Flow Simulation** models the heat transfer both in fluids and in solids. Convection coefficients governing heat transfer between fluids and solids are found from fluid flow conditions. This is very different from a **Thermal** analysis with **Simulation** where convection coefficient must be known.

As we can see, there is an overlap between **Simulation** and **Flow Simulation**: both can do thermal analysis of solids. However, **Flow Simulation** is not intended for thermal analysis of solids; it does it only to the extent necessary to solve thermal conditions present in the analyzed fluid flow.

**Flow Simulation** can be interfaced in different ways with **Thermal** and structural (**Static**, **Nonlinear**) analyses available in **Simulation** (Figure 14-1).

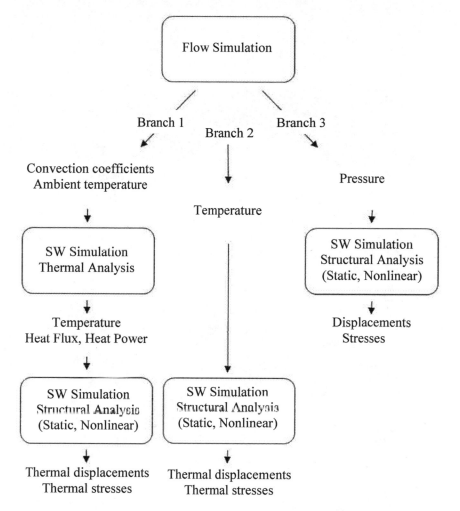

Figure 14-1: Interfacing between Flow Simulation and SOLIDWORKS Simulation.

*If only thermal displacements or stresses are required, it is preferred to follow the right branch (Branch 2).Branch 3 is outside the scope of this book; we won't explore it.*

We should point out that **Flow Simulation** is a tool of flow analysis and is not intended for thermal analysis in solids. It is preferable to use **Flow Simulation** to find convection coefficients, transfer them to a **Thermal** analysis, then use the **Thermal** analysis to find temperature and everything else describing heat transfer. This may be followed by the analysis of thermal stresses in a **Static** or **Nonlinear** analysis. This process is shown in the left branch in Figure 14-1.

A simple assembly model ELBOW (Figure 14-2) will serve to introduce the **Finite Volumes** method used in **Flow Simulation**.

Full model view

Fluid in                                                    Fluid out

Cavity where fluid
flow occurs

Cross-section view

Plug                                                        Plug

Figure 14-2: ELBOW assembly model consists of a square tube and two plugs.

*Two plugs make the model "water-tight."*

The flow of fluid happens here in the space (cavity) inside the solid model, not in the solid model itself. Definition of the space when fluid flow occurs requires plugging up the model as shown in Figure 14-2. In fluid flow analysis, solid geometry is used only to define the space where fluid flow occurs (inside the cavity, around a solid or both). In our case the flow is inside; therefore, only the inside faces of the cavity matter for analysis. As we mentioned earlier, solid geometry is considered in flow analysis only if heat transfer in fluids and solids is specified in the analysis settings. The combined heat transfer in fluids and solids is called **conjugate heat transfer**. It is classified in **Flow Simulation** as an advanced topic. To introduce **Flow Simulation** gradually, the ELBOW example won't include heat transfer.

Using **Finite Volumes,** the space where fluid flow occurs is discretized into cubes parallel to the global coordinate system. If heat transfer in solids is requested in analysis, then solids are also discretized. A **Finite Volumes** mesh, most often referred to as a grid, can be only shown in cross-sections as illustrated in Figure 14-3.

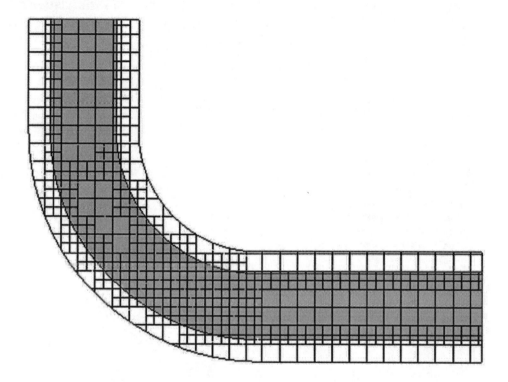

Figure 14-3: Cross sectional through the Finite Volume grid.

*Cells modeling fluid are shaded in this illustration. Cells modeling solid are shown in white and are here only because heat transfer in solids has been requested prior to grid generation. Curvilinear geometry requires a more refined grid of orthogonal cubes to approximate curvature; therefore, smaller cells are located along the rounds.*

*Solid cells will not be present in the analysis that follows. They are shown here for illustration purposes only.*

The grid cells may be classified into three types: fluid, solid and partial. Partial cells are located on boundaries between fluid and solid and include both solid and fluid volume. The size of the cubes depends on the geometry and on the requested level of solution accuracy. Grid refinement is conducted by splitting a cell into eight smaller cells.

Parameters characterizing fluid flow and heat transfer are evaluated in the middle of a cell so modeling of a linear temperature gradient in a solid wall requires at least two layers of cells.

As we said before, the ELBOW model is an introductory exercise in fluid flow analysis with no thermal conditions. First, make sure that **Flow Simulation** is an active add-in (Figure 14-4) and is showing as a tab in the **Command Manager**.

Figure 14-4: SOLIDWORKS Flow Simulation Add-in must be active.

*Make sure the Flow Simulation tab is available in the Command Manager.*

Start a new **Flow Simulation** project using a **Wizard** as shown in Figure 14-5. The **Wizard** will walk you through steps necessary to set up a flow analysis project.

(2) Select Wizard

(1) Select Flow Simulation

Figure 14-5: Starting a Flow Simulation Project using a Wizard.

*The Wizard will walk you through the steps necessary to define a project which is an equivalent to a "Study" in Simulation.*

Steps in the project definition are shown in Figures 14-6 through 14-12.

Figure 14-6: Step 1: Project name definition.

*The project windows are more informative if you keep the Navigator panel open. The panel on the right lists all the steps to be performed. Click Next or Back to move through the steps.*

Figure 14-7: Step 2: Unit system.

*Accept the default SI system of units.*

Select Internal

Schematic
illustration of
**internal flow;**
fluid flows in a
cavity of a solid
body

Step 3

Figure 14-8: Step 3: Analysis type.

*Select the Internal type of analysis; do not select Heat conduction in solids in this exercise.*

Click Add to accept the default fluid: Water

Step4

Figure 14-9: Step 4: Default Fluid.

*Select Water from the list of pre-defined fluid by double clicking it.*

Figure 14-10: Step 5: Wall conditions.

*Adiabatic wall means no heat exchange; do not change anything here.*

Figure 14-11: Step 6: Initial Conditions.

*Do not change anything here. The example we are setting up is a steady state fluid flow; velocity parameters will be found by solver.*

Click Finish to exit Wizard

**Figure 14-12: Step 7 and Step 8: Results and geometry Resolution and Finish.**

*Accept the default resolution level 3. This controls the level of grid refinement performed during the solution process. It is comparable to mesh refinement in FEA.*

A **Flow Simulation** project tab has been added and the CAD model view now shows the **Computational Domain**. Notice that it does not include solid walls because we have not selected heat transfer in solids.

Flow Simulation project tab

Project 01

Right click to hide or display the Computational Domain

This toggles the display of CAD geometry

Figure 14-13: The computational domain is parallel to the global coordinate system.

*Practice hiding and showing the CAD model and the Computational Domain.*

Familiarize yourself with the **Flow Simulation** Command Manager which is now fully active.

We'll now set up conditions in the inlet and outlet defining fluid flow. Right-click **Boundary Conditions** and select **Insert Boundary Conditions**, then follow the steps in Figure 14-14.

Figure 14-14: Setting up boundary conditions on the inlet side.

*Notice that a call-out is added to the face where the boundary condition has been defined. Instead of using Select Other technique you may use cross-section view to select the desired face directly.*

Follow the steps in Figure 14-15 to complete the fluid flow definition on the outlet side.

Figure 14-15: Setting up boundary conditions on the outlet side.

*Accept the default pressure and the default temperature. Temperature has no importance in this analysis.*

The last step before running the solution is the setup of **Goals** for the project. These are flow parameters which are of interest and, therefore, we ask the solver to consider them when it performs the convergence check.

Right click Goals
Select Global Goals

Select Avg. velocity as the parameter of interest

Figure 14-16: Definition of solution Goals.

*Only one Global Goal is selected as parameter of interest.*

The flow analysis in ELBOW is for demonstration purpose only; therefore, we define only one **Goal**.

Right-click **Project 01** in either of two places shown in Figure 14-17 and select **Run**.

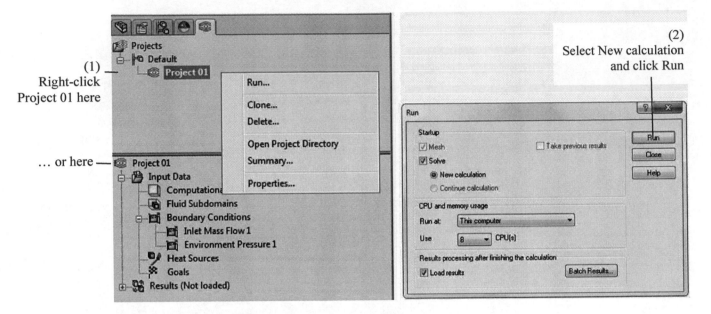

Figure 14-17: Running the solution of Project 01.

*Starting the solution requires two steps as shown above.*

Solution progress may be monitored using the **Solver** window shown in Figure 14-18.

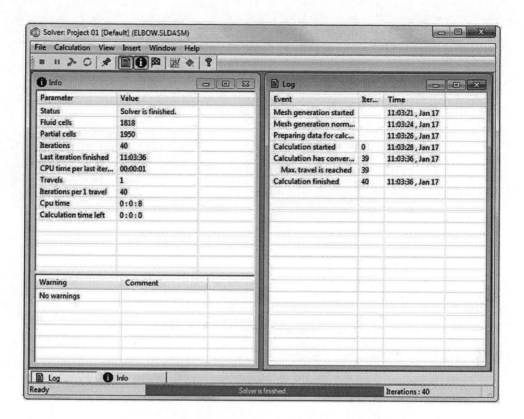

Figure 14-18: Solver window.

*Use Info and Log windows to monitor the solution progress.*

Closing the **Solver** window allows you to access the results of the flow analysis (Figure 14-19).

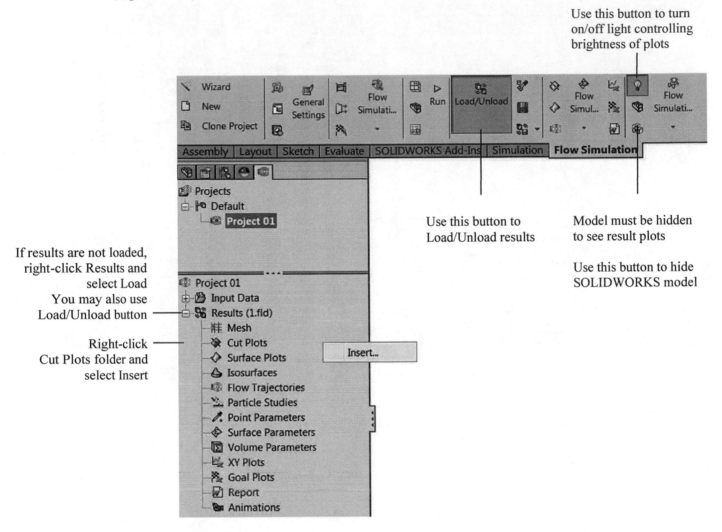

Use this button to turn on/off light controlling brightness of plots

Use this button to Load/Unload results

Model must be hidden to see result plots

Use this button to hide SOLIDWORKS model

If results are not loaded, right-click Results and select Load
You may also use Load/Unload button

Right-click Cut Plots folder and select Insert

Figure 14-19: Result folders.

*Right-click the desired folder and select Insert to add a plot of the desired type.*

In this introductory exercise we limit the analysis of results to a quick review of pressure (Figure 14-20) and velocity plots (Figure 14-21).

Figure 14-20: Pressure plot; a very low pressure drop can be seen.

*To construct this plot, make selections as indicated.*

Hide the above plot before constructing the next one.

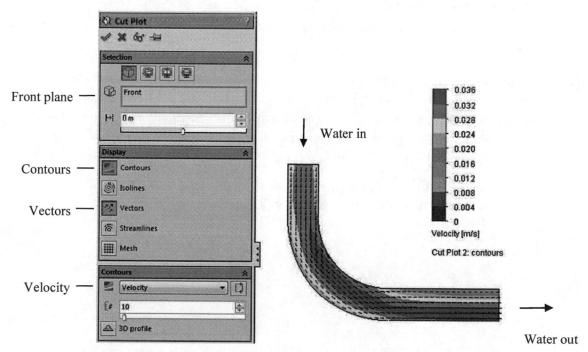

Figure 14-21: A velocity plot illustrates a non-uniform velocity distribution caused by the curvature of ELBOW.

*To construct this plot, make selections as indicated.*

To complete this review and prepare yourself for the next exercise construct a mesh plot as shown in Figure 14-22.

Figure 14-22: Mesh plot.

*To construct this plot, make selections as indicated.*

Remember to review only one plot at a time or else plots will be overlaid; hide pressure and velocity plots prior to viewing the mesh plot. Review the mesh plot in Figure 14-22 and notice that the cavity where flow occurs is meshed and the surrounding walls are not. This is because heat flow through solids has not been requested in this exercise, so there was no need to mesh the solid geometry.

Remember to hide CAD geometry using **Display Model Geometry** command in the **Flow Simulation** Command Manager (Figure 14-13).

We now move to a problem where fluid flow is accompanied by heat flow; this is a **Conjugate** heat transfer problem. Open assembly model MANIFOLD shown in Figure 14-23. Our objective is to find thermal stresses in this exhaust manifold of a three cylinder engine. Along the way we'll have to analyze fluid flow to find convective boundary condition between flowing gas and solid model. Convection boundary conditions on the outside faces are assumed to be known.

Figure 14-23: MANIFOLD 040 assembly model.

*Plugs on three inlets and one outlet are shown.*

The model is made watertight by plugging up three inlets and one outlet. The following parameters define the flow analysis and structural analysis conditions. We assume a steady state flow.

**Flow conditions:**
Flow in: 0.02kg/s into each inlet, gas (air) temperature 773.15K, approx. pressure 1atm
Flow out: atmospheric pressure
Convection coefficient on all outside walls: 20W/(m²K)
Prescribed temperature on the face attached to the engine block: 353.15K

**Structural conditions:**
The face attached to the engine block may expand but must remain flat.
Thermal loads (temperatures) from a Thermal study following Branch 1 in Figure 14-1
or
Thermal loads (temperatures) directly from Flow Simulation following Branch 2 in Figure 14-1

Keep it in mind that that prescribed temperature boundary conditions override convection boundary conditions.

Use the **Wizard** to create a **Flow Simulation** project, and call it *Project 02*. We show only the windows that are different from the ELBOW project.

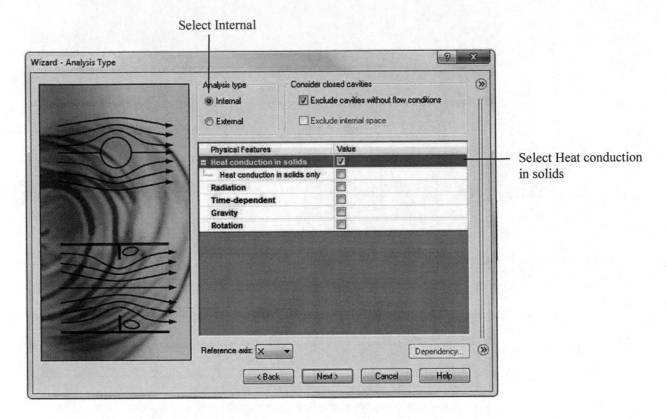

Figure 14-24: Analysis type.

*Select Heat conduction in solids.*

Figure 14-25: Default fluid.

*Select Air as the fluid. Use the list of Pre-Defined fluids to make this selection. Scroll the list to find Air.*

Gray Cast Iron selected

Figure 14-26: Default Solid.

*Select Gray Cast Iron from the "Solids in the model" list.*

20W/(m²K) convection coefficient and 293.2K ambient temperature selected

Figure 14-27: Wall Conditions.

*Define a Heat transfer coefficient of 20W/(m²K) as the default convection coefficient on the outside walls. This "imposed" definition is required because fluid flow on the outside of MANIFOLD is not modeled.*

Accept default settings for the remaining steps of the **Wizard**. Having completed the steps in the **Wizard** we proceed as follows:

Right-click the **Solid Materials** folder in *Project 02* to open the **Solid Material** definition window as shown in Figure 14-28. Select all four plugs from the fly-out menu and assign an **Insulator** material from the list of pre-defined materials to them.

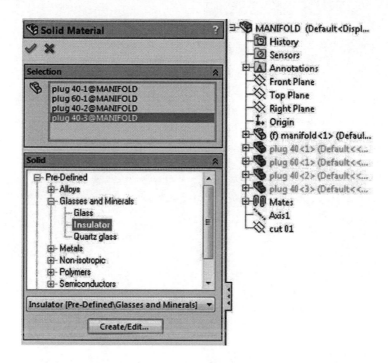

Figure 14-28: Material definition of plugs.

*Material is defined as Insulator to prevent plugs from participating in the heat transfer.*

Plugs do not exist as real parts. They are added to the model to make it "water-tight." By defining their material as **Insulator**, we exclude plugs from heat transfer analysis.

Define flow boundary conditions on the three inlets as shown in Figure 14-29. Flow in one inlet is 0.02kg/s; if you want to define flow boundary conditions on all three inlets at the same time, you must define it as 0.06kg/s. Enter the pressure as 1atm and temperature as 773.15K. 1atm pressure will be converted automatically to SI units.

Figure 14-29: Flow boundary conditions on three inlets.

*This mass flow corresponds to a two stroke, three cylinder engine with a displacement of 850cm³ running at 4000RPM.*

The approximate inlet pressure is 1atm; this is because we do not expect to see much of a pressure drop in the manifold. Repeat the definition of boundary conditions for the remaining two inlets.

Define flow boundary conditions on the outlet as shown in Figure 14-30.

Pressure openings

Accept default
parameters of
Environment pressure

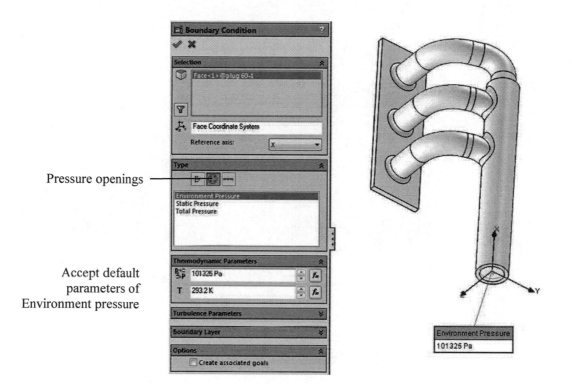

Figure 14-30: Flow boundary conditions on the outlet.

*Accept default parameters of environment pressure because exhaust gases exit to the environment.*

Define a prescribed temperature of 353.15K on the face where the manifold attaches to the engine block as shown in Figure 14-31.

Figure 14-31: A prescribed temperature of the flat face that attaches to the engine block.

*A prescribed temperature boundary condition overrides convective boundary conditions coefficient; this is why the convection coefficient definition window is disabled in the above Boundary Condition window.*

The prescribed temperature boundary condition overrides convection boundary conditions that have been defined on all external faces (Figure 14-27). This override applies only to this face; everywhere else the convection coefficient remains unchanged at $20W/(m^2K)$.

Define the solution **Goals** as the average and the maximum velocity, and the average and maximum heat flux (Figure 14-32).

Average and maximum Velocity

Average and maximum Heat Flux

Average and maximum Temperature in Solid

Figure 14-32: Definition of solution Goals.

*Average and Maximum Temperature in Solid are selected because we are particularly interested in thermal effects present in this problem. This illustration has been modified in a graphics program to show all goals without scrolling.*

The fluid flow is now fully defined and you may run the solution. Before proceeding with thermal and thermal stress analyses, review the results of the **Flow Simulation**. In addition to the steps explained in the ELBOW exercise, you may want to visualize flow trajectories. Right-click **Flow Trajectories** in the **Results** folder and follow the steps shown in Figure 14-33. Show trajectories and the model at the same time by adjusting the model transparency. This is done with the **Set Model Transparency** command located under **Display Model Geometry** in **Flow Simulation** Command Manager (Figure 14-13).

Right-click, make sure you select the inside face

Velocity [m/s]

Flow Trajectories 1

Figure 14-33: Plot of flow trajectories.

*Right-click the face on the outlet or all three inlets faces; accept all defaults. Set model transparency to 0.5.*

Figure 14-33 shows flow trajectories and the transparent model. The transparency and other graphics settings may be adjusted from the menu shown in Figure 14-34 or using the button directly under the **Show/Hide** CAD geometry button.

The plot of flow trajectories is for information only; it is not directly related to the analysis of thermal stresses which is the objective of this exercise.

Figure 14-34: Figure 14-34: Flow Simulation graphics settings and Load/Unload command can be found in the Flow Simulation Command Manager.

*Experiment with all graphics display settings; notice that some items are not available if results are not loaded.*

Management of results in **Flow Simulation** is different from the system used in **Simulation**. Results files are named by numbers not directly associated with project name. They are located in folders with the same numerical names. Results may be loaded or unloaded using the **Load/Unload** command in the **Flow Simulation** Command Manager window (Figure 14-34) or through the **Flow Simulation** Feature Manager as shown in Figure 14-35.

Figure 14-35: Load/Unload in Flow Simulation Feature Manager window.

*The load command will load default results associated with the project. You may also load other results selecting Load from File.*

In preparation for the analysis of thermal results, review the temperature results produced by **Flow Simulation**. Right-click **Surface Plots** in the **Results** folder and select outside faces to create a temperature plot as shown in Figure 14-36.

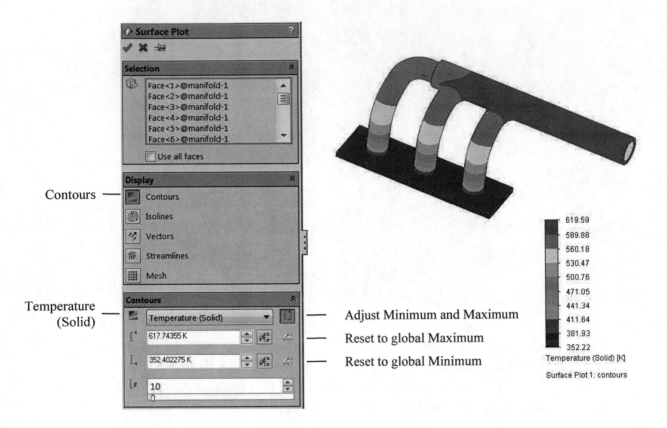

Figure 14-36: Temperature of the outside faces; model is hidden.

*The color legend may be selected and moved with a left mouse click. In Flow Simulation, temperature can only be shown on surfaces or cross-sections; it cannot be show in the volumes.*

**Flow Simulation** has created all the results we need for structural and thermal analyses. Refer to Figure 14-37 for information on how to find the **Flow Simulation** project results.

Load/unload results

**2.fld** file is here

Results (2.fld)

Results are stored in fld file.
The file shown here is **2.fld**

Files and folders in MANIFOLD.SLDASM folder.
The result file **2.fld** is located in folder 2

Figure 14-37: Location of results of Flow Simulation project.

*Results may be loaded and unloaded using the Load/Unload button.*

*Your results file may be numbered differently*

Results of **Flow Simulation** must be transferred to **Simulation** as shown in Figure 14-38. Save the model before and after exporting the results.

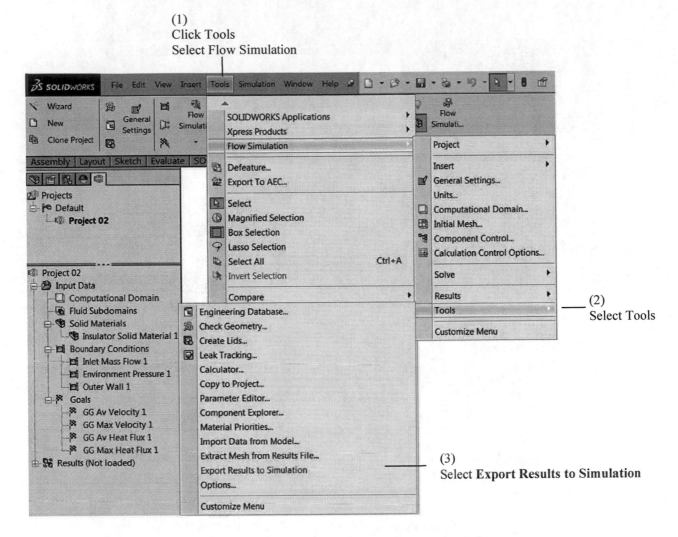

Figure 14-38: Transferring results from Flow Simulation to Simulation.

*Each step indicated above opens a new menu. Save the model before and after exporting results to Simulation.*

Notice that when you move to **Simulation**, the model display and its visibility as well as display of **Flow Simulation** results plots are still affected by settings in **Flow Simulation**. Learn how to move between windows of **SOLIDWORKS** Feature Manager, **Simulation** studies and **Flow Simulation** projects.

Hide the plugs from view (but do not suppress them) in **SOLIDWORKS** Feature manager and create a **Thermal** study *01 Thermal*.

We'll now follow Branch 1 in Figure 14-1. In *01 Thermal* study properties select **Include fluid convection effects from SOLIDWORKS Flow Simulation** and select the correct **Flow Simulation** project file as shown in Figure 14-37. **Thermal** study properties are shown in Figure 14-39.

Select **Include fluid convection effects**

Select the **Flow Simulation** results file.
Here the results file is **2.fld** as shown in Figure 14-37

Figure 14-39: Importing convection coefficients from Flow Simulation results to Simulation.

*If you have more than one Flow Simulation project, make sure to select the correct Flow Simulation results file.*

Importing **Flow Simulation** results as shown in Figure 14-39 only brings the convective boundary conditions that have been calculated in **Flow Simulation** into the **Thermal** study. Convection coefficients and ambient temperatures that have been "imposed" in a project definition (Figure 14-27) must be defined in the **Thermal** study. Prescribed temperatures (Figure 14-31) also must be defined.

Exclude all plugs from the analysis and define a convection coefficient of 20W/(m²K) with an ambient temperature of 293.2K on all external faces. This corresponds to the **Wall Conditions** defined in **Flow Simulation** (Figure 14-27).

Define a prescribed temperature of 80°C on the face contacting the engine block. This corresponds to **Wall Conditions** defined in **Flow Simulation** (Figure 14-31).

Mesh the model using a **Curvature Controlled Mesh** with 5mm element size and 16 elements in a circle.

Complete set-up of *Thermal 01* study is shown in Figure 14-40.

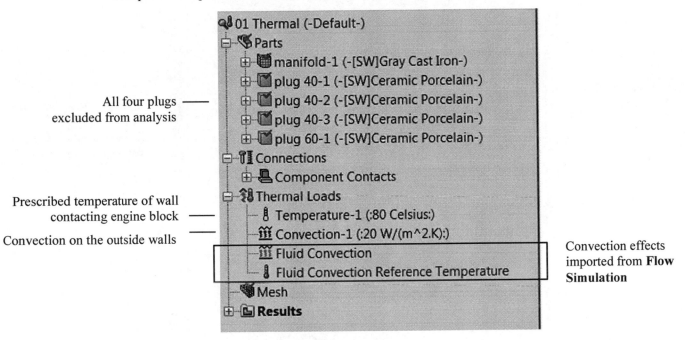

All four plugs excluded from analysis

Prescribed temperature of wall contacting engine block

Convection on the outside walls

Convection effects imported from **Flow Simulation**

Figure 14-40: Thermal 01 study ready to run.

*All plugs are hidden in SOLIDWORKS and excluded from analysis in 01 Thermal study.*

Thermal conditions imported from **Flow Simulation** can be reviewed as shown in Figure 14-41.

Right-click "Fluid Convection" imported from **Flow Simulation**

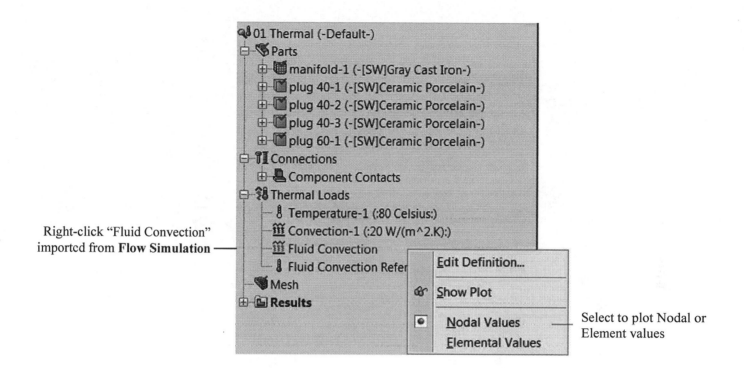

Select to plot Nodal or Element values

Figure 14-41: Displaying convection coefficients imported from Flow Simulation.

*The Fluid Convection Reference Temperature may be displayed the same way.*

Displaying **Fluid Convection** and **Fluid Convection Reference Temperature** will work only if the model has already been meshed.

In this project, the imported convection coefficients and reference temperatures are for inside faces of the manifold. Since section plots are not available for these types of plots, the review of plots is limited to openings on the side of inlets and outlet.

Run the solution of *01 Thermal* study and display a **Temperature** plot (Figure 14-42).

Figure 14-42: Temperature results from Thermal analysis.

*This plot is very similar to the temperature in the solids plot in Flow Simulation (Figure 14-36).*

The difference between temperature results for solids reported by **Flow Simulation** and **Thermal** analysis in **Simulation** is caused by the error of translation fluid convection effects from Flow Simulation to Simulation and by discretization error in both applications.

Temperature results from **Flow Simulation** are available for surfaces only; **Thermal** analysis provides plots showing results for the entire volume. You may now use these **Thermal** analysis results to analyze heat flux, heat power etc. This wouldn't be possible within **Flow Simulation** which is not intended for analysis of solids.

We now proceed to the analysis of thermal stress. Create a static study called *01 Thermal stress*. In the properties of this study specify **Temperature from thermal study** *01 Thermal* (Figure 14-43). Exclude all plugs from the analysis and copy the mesh from *01 Thermal* study.

Temperatures from thermal study *01 Thermal*

Reference temperature at zero strain 293.2C

Figure 14-43: Properties of 01 Thermal Stress study.

*The reference temperature at zero strain corresponds to the temperature of the external fluid defined in Figure 14-27.*

As in any structural analysis the model must have proper restraints. The MANIFOLD model, even though it is loaded with self-balanced thermal loads must still be supported to eliminate all **Rigid Body Motions (RBMs)**. We'll define restraints to eliminate all **RBMs** without interfering with the model's thermal expansion.

For clarity, the restraints definition will be split into three steps:

**Step 1**

The face where prescribed temperature was defined is attached to the engine block; it may expand along with it but it must remain flat. This is modeled by eliminating translations in the direction normal to the face and once done leaves the model with three **RBMs**: two translations and one rotation. Step 1 can be accomplished, for example, with a **Roller/Slider** restraint.

**Step 2**

One vertex (corner) on the face is **Fixed**; it restrains translation but not rotation; remember that structural solid elements have only translational degrees of freedom. This still leaves one **RBM**.

**Step 3**

A vertex on the opposite side of the wall is restrained in one direction, and this leaves the model with no **RBMs**.

Restraints are shown in Figure 14-44.

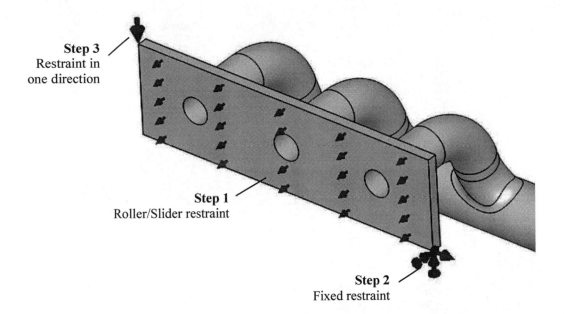

Figure 14-44: Restraints in 01 Thermal Stress study.

*The Roller/Slider assures flatness of the face. Fixed and One direction are here only to eliminate RBMs. Alternatively you could use Soft springs option in study properties to eliminate RBMs.*

Run study *01 Thermal stress* and review **P1 stress** results (Figure 14-45). Notice that von Mises stress must not be used here because MANIFOLD model material is Gray Iron. This is a **brittle** material and its yield strength is not defined. Von Mises stress is applicable to the analysis of ductile materials but not brittle materials.

Figure 14-45: P1 stress results from *01 Thermal Stress* study.

*The locations of stress concentrations are indicated by arrows.*

*Gray Iron tensile strength is 151MPa. The factor of safety is 151/45=3.4.*

*This is a static factor of safety and does not take into consideration fatigue effects.*

Review stress results with mesh showing to see that element size should be decreased where stress concentrations are present. We use this mesh to make the model solve faster. It is recommended to repeat this exercise using a more refined mesh.

We conclude the MANIFOLD exercise by demonstrating the analysis along Branch 2 (Figure 14-1). Copy study *01 Thermal* stress into *02 Thermal stress*. Modify the properties of *02 Thermal stress* study as shown in Figure 14-46.

Temperatures from **Flow Simulation** ——

Figure 14-46: Properties of 02 Thermal Stress study.

*Temperatures are imported directly from the Flow Simulation project.*

The change in the study property is the only modification required in study *02 Thermal stress*. Run the study solution and review P1 stress results (Figure 14-47).

Figure 14-47: P1 stress results from *02 Thermal stress* study.

*The locations of stress concentrations are indicated by arrows.*

*Gray Iron tensile strength is 151MPa. The factor of safety is 151/44=3.4.*

*This is a static factor of safety and does not take into consideration fatigue effects.*

Thermal stress results from studies *01 Thermal stress* and *02 Thermal stress* are almost identical. We have demonstrated two ways of interfacing between **Flow Simulation**, **Thermal,** and **Static** (Figure 14-1) in this introductory exercise. If thermal analysis in solids is required you have to follow Branch 1. If thermal stresses only are required, then direct interfacing along Branch 2 is easier and faster.

You may want to extend this exercise to include pressure effects from **Flow Simulation** in a **Static** analysis but this would be outside of the scope of this book.

*Notes:*

# 15: Heat transfer with external fluid flow

## Topics covered

- Using Flow Simulation for finding convection coefficients in external fluid flow
- Interfacing between Flow Simulation and Thermal analysis

## Project description

Figure 15-1 explains the differences between internal and external fluid flow.

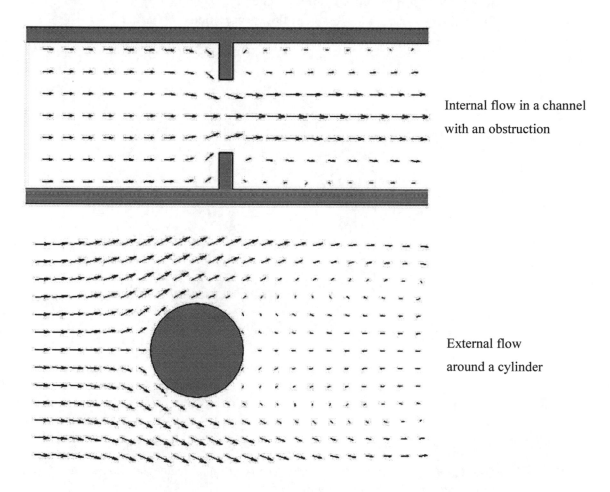

Internal flow in a channel
with an obstruction

External flow
around a cylinder

Figure 15-1: Internal and external fluid flow.

*Velocity vectors are shown in both illustrations.*

The illustrations in Figure 15-1 were prepared using models INTERNAL FLOW and EXTERNAL FLOW. These models come with **Flow Simulation** projects defined so it is easy to use these models to replicate the above plots. The INTERNAL FLOW model uses automatically created plugs which have not been used in the previous chapter.

To study heat transfer in the presence of external fluid flow we'll analyze a brass sphere submerged in slow flowing water. The heat power of the sphere is 1000W. The temperature of the cooling water is 293.2K; water is under atmospheric pressure and the flow velocity is 0.1m/s.

Open part model BALL15 which is shown in Figure 15-2. The same figure also shows the **Computational Domain** automatically defined by the **Flow Simulation** wizard when external flow is specified.

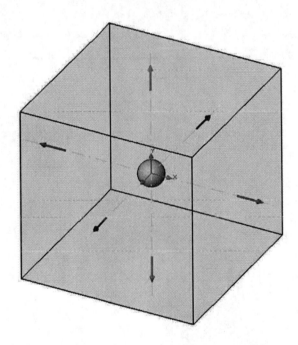

Figure 15-2: Model BALL15 and the Computational Domain.

*The Computational Domain extends to the region where the external flow is no longer disturbed by the immersed object.*

Use the **Wizard** to define a **Flow Simulation** project. Figures 15-3 through 15-9 show windows corresponding to steps performed by the **Wizard**. Compare them carefully with the **Wizard** steps from the previous chapter where we analyzed internal flow.

Figure 15-3: Step 1: Project name definition.

*You may move though Wizard windows using the Next and Back buttons or by selecting steps from the Navigator menu on the right.*

Figure 15-4: Step 2: Unit system.

*Accept the default SI system of units.*

Select External

Schematic
illustration of
**external flow;**
fluid flows
around a solid
body

Step 3

Figure 15-5: Step 3: Analysis type.

*Select the External type of analysis; select Heat conduction in solids.*

Step 4

Figure 15-6: Step 4: Default fluid.

*Select water from the list of pre-defined fluids.*

Figure 15-7: Step 5: Default Solid.

*Select Brass from "Solids in the model."*

Figure 15-8: Step 6: Wall Conditions.

*Do not change anything here; the ball surface is assumed to be perfectly smooth.*

Flow velocity in X direction is 0.1m/s

Step 7

Figure 15-9: Step 7: Initial and Ambient Conditions; flow velocity in X direction is 0.1m/s

*This defines the velocity of the external flow.*

Step 8

Step 9

Figure 15-10: Step 8 and Step 9: Results and geometry Resolution.

*We select resolution level 6 for precise transfer of convective boundary conditions to Simulation. Click Finish when done. Considering Result resolution is set at 6; be prepared for a long solution time. You may use a lower resolution to speed up the solution.*

Follow the steps shown in Figure 15-11 to define the 1000W heat power generated in the entire volume of the model.

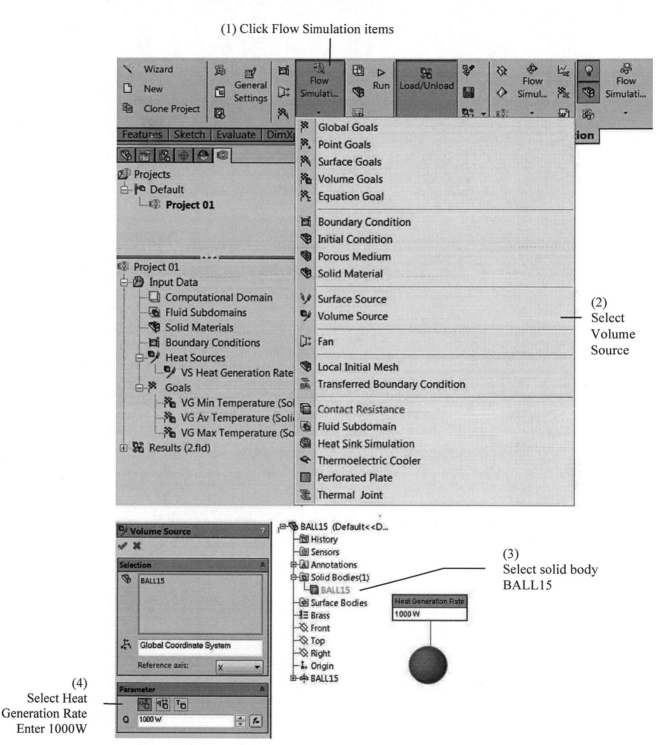

Figure 15-11: Definition of heat power.

*Heat Generation Rate applies heat power to the entire volume of the selected solid body.*

The objective of this analysis is finding the temperature of the ball cooled by the flow of water. Therefore, create Goals as shown in Figure 15-12.

Figure 15-12: Definition of analysis goals.

*The minimum, the average and the maximum temperature will be used in the convergence check.*

Run the solution and observe the convergence process as shown in Figure 15-13. Be prepared for a long solution time.

Click Insert Goal Plot to see live convergence graphs

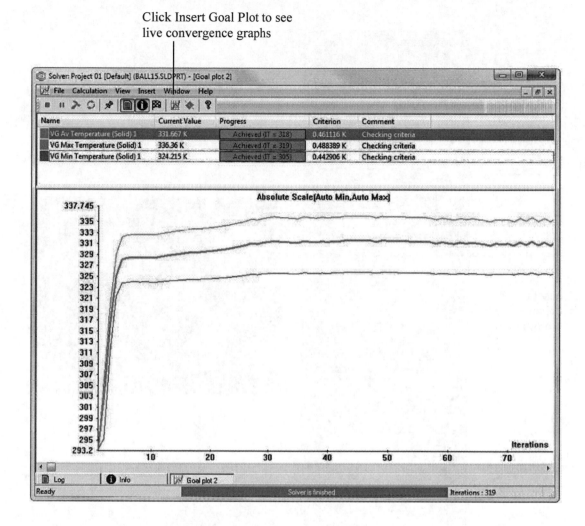

Figure 15-13: Monitoring solution progress in the Solver window.

*Review other options available in the Solver window.*

Analysis of water flow is not an objective of this analysis; still, you may look at some results pertaining to flow. For example, create a **Cut Plot** of velocities as shown in Figure 15-14.

Figure 15-14: Velocity cut plot definition.

*The plot area has been cropped as shown.*

Define a **Cut Plot** showing temperature in the solid as shown in Figure 15-15.

Figure 15-15: Temperature in the cross section of the ball.

*Notice that the mesh in the solid includes solid cells and partial cells; this may be illustrated better if the mesh in the fluid and in the solid are displayed.*

Hide all **Flow Simulation** plots and display the model geometry.

Export the results of **Flow Simulation** to **Simulation** as explained in Figure 14-38. Remember to save the model before and after exporting the results.

In the **Thermal** study properties created within **Simulation**, select **Include fluid convection effects from SOLIDWORKS Flow Simulation**. Make sure to select the correct \*.fld file (Figure 14-37).

Define a **Heat Power** of 1000W in the volume and mesh the model with the default mesh.

All thermal conditions necessary to run the study have now been set-up. You may review the convective boundary conditions imported from **Flow Simulation** as shown in Figure 15-16.

Right-click
Fluid Convection.
Select Show Plot

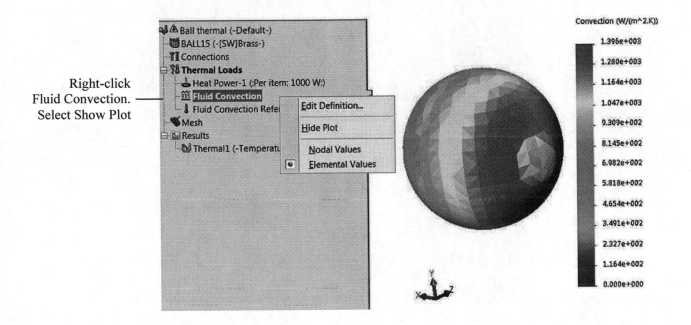

Figure 15-16: convection boundary conditions imported from Flow Simulation.

*The somewhat irregular shape of the fringes is a result of discretization error in Flow Simulation and the error of translation from Flow Simulation to the Thermal study in Simulation.*

In continuation of the plot review in Figure 15-16, display element values of the **Fluid Convection** plot. Once this is done, review the plot of **Fluid Convection Reference Temperature**.

Run the solution of the **Thermal** study and display the temperature plot (Figure 15-17).

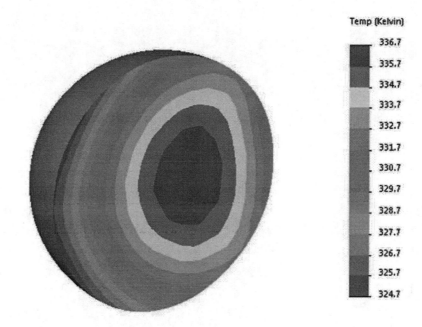

Figure 15-17: Temperature in the cross section of the ball.

*Section clipping makes this plot directly comparable to the plot in Figure 15-15.*

Having obtained results in a **Thermal** analysis, you may wish to proceed to a detailed analysis of thermal conditions in the ball.

This exercise offers a good opportunity to study the effect of grid density in **Flow Simulation** on the accuracy of flow simulation and the accuracy of transfer of convective boundary conditions from Flow **Simulation** to **Thermal** analysis in **Simulation**, but this falls out of the scope of this book.

*Notes:*

# 16: Radiative Heat Transfer

## Topics covered

❑ Radiative heat transfer problem solvable with Thermal Study in SOLIDWORKS Simulation and with Flow Simulation

## Project description

A graphite sphere produces a 2000W heat power in its volume. The heat is radiated out of the ball into space; some of the heat is reflected by the steel reflector. The ball and reflector are in a vacuum, therefore there is no convection involved in the heat transfer. This presents a **Surface to surface** radiation problem with an **Open system** and is easy to solve with a **Thermal** study in **SOLIDWORKS Simulation**. What makes this problem interesting is that it can also be solved with Flow Simulation. Solving the same problem with **Finite Volume Method (FV)** implemented in **Flow Simulation** and with **Finite Element Method (FEM or FEA)** implemented in **Thermal** study in **SOLIDWORKS Simulation** offers a comparison between these two numerical techniques and the way they have been implemented into commercial analysis systems.

Open assembly model RADIATIVE HEAT TRANSFER shown in Figure 16-1.

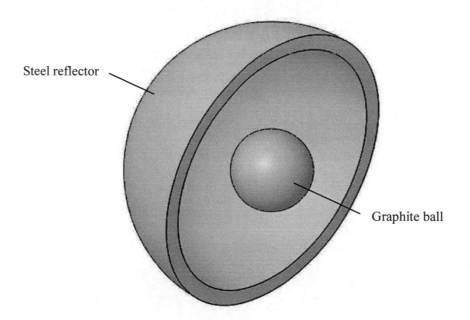

Steel reflector

Graphite ball

Figure 16-1: The graphite ball is partially surrounded by a steel reflector.

*The assembly is in a vacuum; therefore, convective heat transfer does not take place.*

## *Procedure*

We'll first solve this problem with **Flow Simulation**, then we'll solve it the "standard way" with a **Thermal** study, matching as closely as possible the modeling assumptions introduced in the **Flow Simulation** study. Results of both studies should be close but not identical.

Use the **Flow Simulation Wizard** to set up the project as shown in Figures 16-2 through 16-7.

Figure 16-2: Steps 1and 2: Project Name and Unit System.

*These windows are self-explanatory.*

External analysis

Heat conduction in solids and only in solids

Radiative heat transfer to be considered with an "Environment temperature" (ambient) of 293.2K

Figure 16-3: Step 3: Analysis Type.

*Make selections as shown above to activate radiative heat transfer.*

Default material

Figure 16-4: Step 4: Default solid.

*Make the Reflector material, AISI321, the default material.*

Click the selection button to open the Engineering Database window below

Select Whitebody wall

Figure 16-5: Step 5: Wall conditions.

*Select Whitebody as the default wall condition.*

The **Whitebody** default wall conditions defined in Step 5 means that the radiative heat reaching the walls is completely reflected. No portion of heat is absorbed by the walls.

Figure 16-6: Step 6: Initial and Ambient Conditions.

*Accept the default Initial solid temperature of 293.2K.*

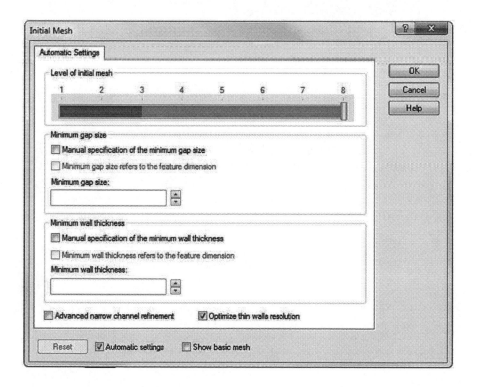

Figure 16-7: Step 7: Results and Geometry Resolution.

*Select a level 8 resolution for a more accurate discretization of curvilinear geometry. Click Finish to exit the Wizard.*

Review the **Computational Domain** as explained in Figure 16-8.

Figure 16-8: The automatically created Computational Domain can be modified using the Computational Domain window.

*Right-click the Computational Domain folder in the Flow Simulation study to activate the window shown on the right. The values shown above are round-offs of the default computational domain to one decimal place.*

Modification of the Computational Domain is not required in this exercise.

Having completed the initial steps with the project **Wizard**, modify the model display as explained in Figure 16-9.

Right-click the project title (here FVM 01) and select Hide Global Coordinate System

Right-click Computational Domain and select Hide

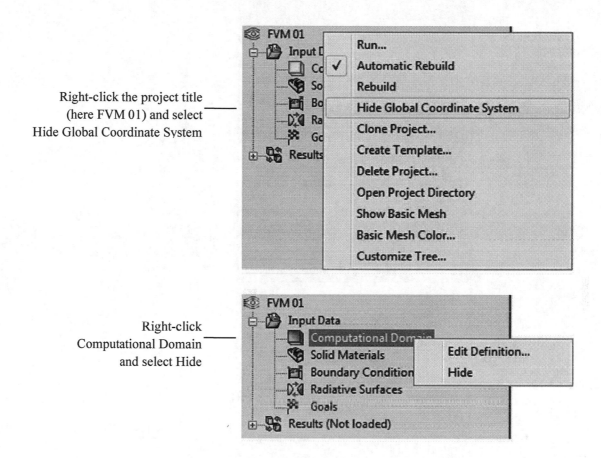

Figure 16-9: Hide the Global Coordinate System and the Computational Domain.

*These are "cosmetic" changes to improve clarity of plots.*

Define material of the graphite ball as shown in Figure 16-10.

<u>Figure 16-10: Material assignment.</u>

*Assignment of the reflector material would be redundant because AISI321 has already been assigned as the default material in step 4 of the Wizard (Figure 16-4).*

Now we'll define heat power and radiative properties of the surface of the graphite ball.

Follow the steps in Figure 16-11 to define a **Volume Source**. Follow the steps in Figure 16-12 to define a **Radiative Surface**.

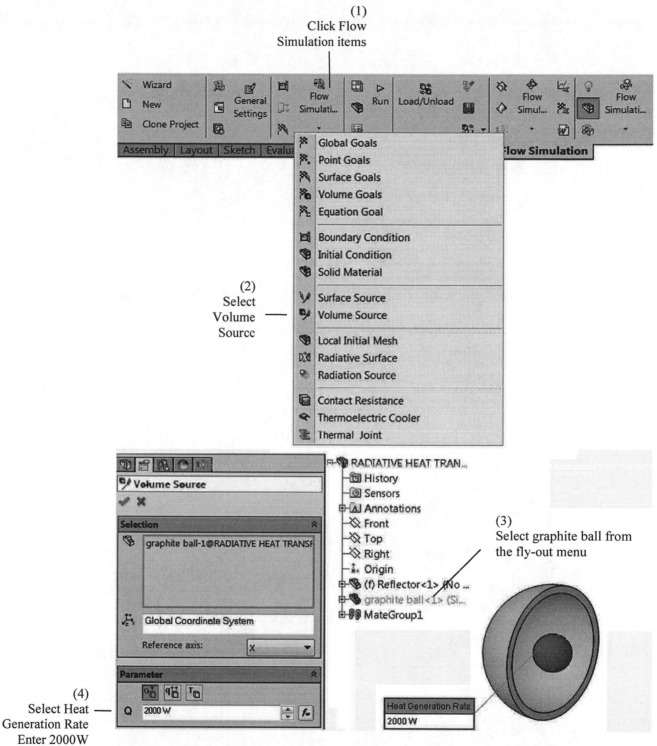

(1)
Click Flow
Simulation items

(2)
Select
Volume
Source

(3)
Select graphite ball from
the fly-out menu

(4)
Select Heat
Generation Rate
Enter 2000W

Figure 16-11: Definition of a Volume Source.

*2000W of heat is generated in the volume of the graphite ball.*

Figure 16-12: Definition of a Radiative surface.

*A Blackbody radiative surface is most efficient in radiating out and absorbing heat in the form of radiation.*

The graphite ball radiates out heat. Some of that heat bounces off the reflector and returns to the graphite ball. Notice that we don't have to define **Radiative Surface** properties for the reflector. This has already been done in step 5 of the **Wizard** (Figure 16-5) where **Whitebody** radiative properties have been applied by defaults to all faces in the model. Those default **Whitebody** conditions have been overwritten on the face of the graphite ball which now has the properties of a **Blackbody**.

The temperature of the reflector will stay at 293.3K as defined in the **Wizard** (Figure 16-6) because the reflector has all **Whitebody** surfaces so no heat will enter it. We are interested in the temperature of the ball; therefore, define **Volume Goals** as shown in Figure 16-13.

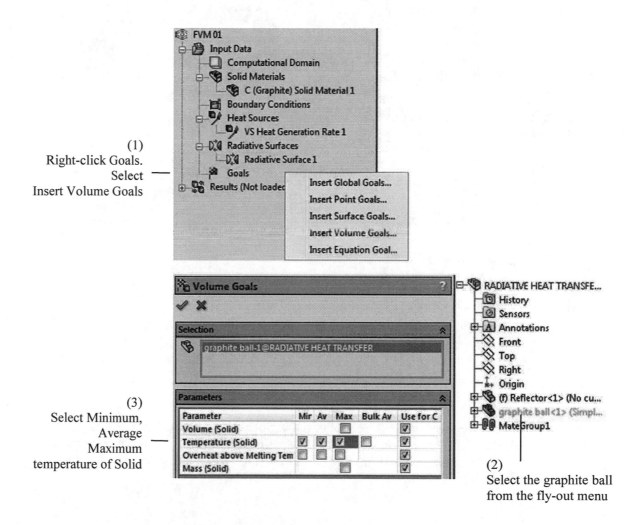

(1)
Right-click Goals.
Select
Insert Volume Goals

(3)
Select Minimum,
Average
Maximum
temperature of Solid

(2)
Select the graphite ball
from the fly-out menu

Figure 16-13: Definition of Goals.

*Minimum, averaged and maximum temperature in solids will be used for checking solution convergence.*

Once the solution completes, create a **Cut Plot** of temperature as shown in Figure 16-14.

(1)
Select
Front cutting plane

(2)
Select Contours

(3)
Select mesh

(4)
Select Temperature
(Solid)

(5)
Define
temperature
range from
1220K to Plot
Maximum

(5)
Click to display
ranges

(6)
Specify 12 levels

Figure 16-14: Temperature results.

*We specify 12 levels in the color legend for consistency with Thermal analysis in Simulation which uses 12 colors by default. The color legend may be moved around with the mouse. White background of the color legend has been added in a graphics program.*

Try to reset the temperature plot to show global minimum and notice that the reflector temperature stays at 293.2K as defined in **Default Wall Conditions**. This is because of the **Whitewall** default surface condition. The reflector does not absorb any heat.

We'll now repeat the analysis using a **Thermal** study in **SOLIDWORKS Simulation**. We'll match analysis assumptions made in **Flow Simulation** as closely as possible.

Create a steady state **Thermal** study and define radiation boundary conditions on the concave face of the reflector as show in Figure 16-15 and on the surface of the ball as shown in Figure 16-16. The "Open system" option checked in both Radiation windows means that some heat is radiated and does not enter either of the parts in the study.

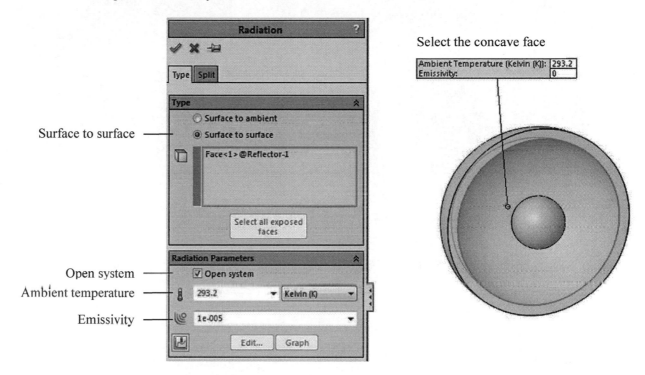

Figure 16-15: Radiation boundary conditions on the face of the reflector.

*Emissivity equal to zero defines Whitebody conditions. Here we enter a very low emissivity 0.00001 because Thermal analysis won't run with emissivity equal zero.*

<u>Figure 16-16: Radiation boundary conditions on the surface of the ball.</u>

*An Emissivity equal to 1 defines Blackbody conditions.*

Define **Heat Power** as shown in Figure 16-17.

Figure 16-17: Heat power definition.

*Select assembly component Heat Sphere from the fly-out menu.*

Select the Reflector from the fly-out menu (not shown here)

Prescribed temperature

Figure 16-18: Temperature definition.

*The temperature pointer appears to point to the graphite ball but it points to the origin of the coordinate system of the reflector.*

We assign a **Temperature** to the Reflector (Figure 16-17) only to match the analysis setup in Flow Simulation where the default temperature of 293.2K was defined for all solids in Step 6 of the **Wizard** (Figure 16-6). This prescribed temperature has no impact on the temperature of the ball. The reflector serves only to reflect heat, and due to **Whitebody** surface conditions, does not absorb any heat.

Mesh the assembly using the default mesh settings and run the solution. Create a **Temperature** plot and to make it look like the **Flow Simulation** plot; use **Section** plot as s shown in Figure 16-18 and a temperature range from 1200K to the maximum.

Figure 16-19: Temperature results plot.

*Use the Front reference plane as a section plane.*

Temperature results from the **Thermal** study in Figure 16-18 closely match the **Flow Simulation** results shown in Figure 16-14.

*Notes:*

# 17: NAFEMS Benchmarks

## Topics covered

- ❑ Importance of benchmarks
- ❑ One dimensional heat transfer with radiation
- ❑ One dimensional transient heat transfer
- ❑ Two dimensional heat transfer with convection

## Project description

Benchmarks are standard tests which can be applied to any Finite Element system. They are intended for users who are interested in the performance of specific codes. The classic set of benchmarks was first published in 1986 by the National Agency for Finite Element Methods and Standards (NAFEMS – see chapter 20). NAFEMS benchmarks were designed to be a little more "searching" than those typically published by software developers since these naturally intended to demonstrate the favorable performance of a system rather than deficiencies. While those tests were critical, they were not designed in such a way that any competent commercial system would not be able to provide satisfactory results.

In this chapter we will test the performance of **SOLIDWORKS Simulation** in three NAFEMS thermal benchmarks with known analytical solutions. Performance will be evaluated by comparing **SOLIDWORKS Simulation** results with targets (expected results) as specified in each test.

Very simple geometries used in these tests lend themselves to more than one representation. Therefore, these exercises will also serve as a review of finite element modeling techniques available in thermal analysis with **SOLIDWORKS Simulation**.

## Procedure

The thermal T2 tests code performance in steady state thermal analysis. A 1D bar has a constant prescribed temperature of 1000K applied to end A, and radiation to an ambient temperature of 300K to end B. There are no other boundary conditions present, meaning that the bar is insulated and there is no heat generated anywhere; the cross section is uniform (Figure 17-1).

A
Constant temperature
1000K

0.1m

B
Radiation to an
ambient temperature
of 300K

Figure 17-1: Geometry and boundary conditions of test T2.

*Since this is a 1D model, only length needs to be specified.*

Benchmark test T2 specifies material properties as follows:

Conductivity = 55.6W/m/K

Specific heat = 460J/kg/K

Density = 7850kg/m$^3$

Emissivity at boundary B = 0.98

Notice that specific heat and density are not required for steady state thermal analysis.

The target in test T2 is temperature at end B. To pass the test, an FEA program should find this temperature to be equal to 927K.

This very simple geometry can be modeled in a number of ways, either as a 3D or 2D problem. 1D elements are not available in **SOLIDWORKS Simulation**. Therefore, our choice is between 3D and 2D representations.

Should we decide to model this as a 3D problem, any prismatic bar with a uniform cross section along the length could be used (Figure 17-2).

Figure 17-2: Examples of CAD geometry that could be used in a T2 test if 3D models were desired.

*The shape and the area of the cross section are irrelevant in this 1D problem. Any of the above bars can be used as long as it has a length of 0.1m.*

Should we decide to model this as a 2D problem, there is again more than one way to accomplish it. First, a bar with a round cross section could be used to create a 2D axisymmetric model. Second, a bar with a rectangular cross section could be used to create a 2D extruded model (Figure 17-3). Alternatively, a surface geometry could be prepared in **SOLIDWORKS** and treated as an axisymmetric or extruded model in a 2D study.

2D axisymmetric                         2D extruded

Figure 17-3: Examples of CAD geometry that could be used in a T2 test if 2D models were desired.

*Large finite elements are shown for clarity of this illustration. We'll use much smaller elements for analysis.*

For the T2 test, we will use a round bar and treat the problem as 3D. In test T3, which uses identical 1D geometry, we will use a square bar treating this problem as 2D extruded.

Open part model T2 and verify that custom material required in test T2 has been defined. Create a steady state thermal study and apply thermal boundary conditions as shown in Figure 17-4 and Figure 17-5.

Figure 17-4: The boundary condition on side A is a prescribed temperature of 1000K.

*A prescribed temperature is applied to side A. Prescribed temperature symbols are shown.*

Create a custom material with properties specified in benchmark test T2 and apply it to the model. To define a custom material, refer to Figure 7-11.

Surface to ambient

Ambient temperature

Emissivity

View factor

Figure 17-5: The boundary condition on side B is a Radiation Surface to ambient.

*A radiation boundary condition is applied to side B. Enlarged radiation symbols are shown.*

An **Ambient temperature** of 300K is the temperature of a distant enclosure which receives heat radiated out from side B. An **Emissivity** of 0.98 is a material property. This is very close to the emissivity of black body so the material is very good at radiating out heat. To understand the meaning of a **View factor** of 1, take into consideration that **Surface to ambient** radiation is specified and that there is only one face in the model. A **View factor** equal to 1 means that the heat radiated out does not "bounce-off" the face again.

Mesh the model with a default mesh and obtain a solution. Show the **Temperature** plot and probe it as shown in Figure 17-6.

Figure 17-6: Probing shows the temperature on the side where the radiation boundary condition has been defined.

*The probed temperature is 927K.*

Probing shows a temperature of 927K as specified in the benchmark target. This demonstrates the correct performance of **Simulation** in this radiation problem. Try running the same problem with a view factor of less than 1, which makes it more difficult to radiate the heat out. The temperature will then be higher than 927K.

Benchmark test T3 requires a transient thermal analysis.

Figure 17-7: Geometry and boundary conditions of test T3.

*The initial temperature is 0°C.*

Benchmark test T3 specifies material properties as follows:

Conductivity = 35.0W/m/K

Specific heat = 440.5J/kg/K

Density = 7200kg/m³

Model T3.SLDPRT comes with these material properties defined.

Notice that the temperature on side B is a function of time so this is a transient thermal problem; therefore, specific heat and density are the required material properties.

The target in test T3 is a temperature at point C at time t=32s. To pass this benchmark test, the FEA program should find this temperature to be 36.6°C.

Open part model T3 and define a thermal study using 2D simplification (Figure 17-8).

Figure 17-8: The 2D Simplification uses an Extruded 2D representation. Slide thickness is 10mm.

*Show preview is deselected to show solid geometry instead of the 2D section. Any thickness may be entered. The split line is where temperature results will be probed.*

Define study properties as shown in Figure 17-9.

Figure 17-9: Properties of the transient thermal study.

*The transient thermal study will be conducted in 40 steps with time increment of 1s.*

Apply an **Initial Temperature** to faces as shown in Figure 17-10 and a **Prescribed Temperature** to side A as shown in Figure 17-11.

Figure 17-10: Definition of an initial temperature.

*Initial temperature is applied to two faces; there are two faces in the 2D model because of the split line.*

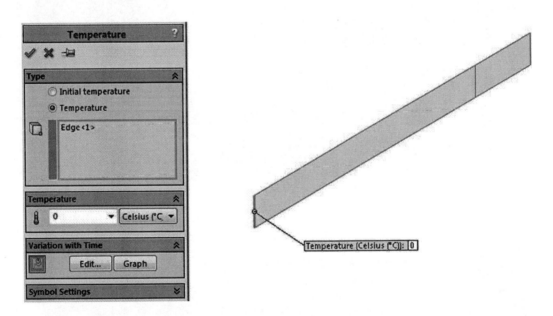

Figure 17-11: Definition of a prescribed temperature on side A.

*Temperature is applied to the edge which represents the face in the 2D model.*

Follow the steps in Figure 17-12 to define a time dependent temperature on side B.

(1)
Select edge on side B

(2)
Enter 1 as a multiplier of values in the Time curve

(3)
Click Edit to open Time curve window

(4)
Copy the table from file T3.xlsx and paste it here, click OK.

Figure 17-12: Definition of the time dependent temperature on side B.

*The time dependency is illustrated by a curve shown in the Preview image.*

The table in file T3.xlsx has been created by tabulating the equation shown Figure 17-7.

Create and apply a new material to the geometry (conductivity = 35.0W/m/K, specific heat = 440.5J/kg/K, density = 7200kg/m³). Mesh the model with the default element size and obtain a solution. To check the target, probe **Temperature** plot as shown in Figure 17-13.

Time step 32

Figure 17-13: Probing temperature plot in location C.

*Make sure the plot is for time 32s and probing is where the split line separates the two faces.*

Probing shows a **Simulation** temperature result of 36.1°C, very close to the benchmark test T3 target of 36.6°C.

Benchmark test T4 is about conductive heat transfer induced by prescribed temperatures and convection to an ambient temperature (Figure 17-14).

Figure 17-14: Geometry and boundary conditions of test T4.

*This is a 2D problem; the thickness is uniform.*

Benchmark test T4 specifies a material conductivity and convection properties as follows:

Conductivity = 52.0W/m/K

Convection = 750W/m²/K

The target in test T4 is temperature at point E. To pass the test, the FEA program should find this temperature to be 18.3°C. Test T4 is a 2D problem.

Open model *T4* and create a thermal study using 2D Simplification as shown in Figure 17-15.

Figure 17-15: 2D Simplification uses Extruded 2D representation.

*This is a 2D extruded problem; the thickness is uniform. Any thickness may be entered. Highlighting of the selected face has been disabled in SOLIDWORKS settings to improve the appearance of this black & white illustration.*

Apply a prescribed temperature and convection boundary conditions as shown in Figure 17-16 and Figure 17-17.

Figure 17-16: Definition of prescribed temperature in test T4.

*Apply a temperature of 100°C to the lower edge. Prescribed temperature symbols are shown.*

Figure 17-17: Definition of convection boundary condition in test T4.

*Apply a convection of 750W/m²/K and an ambient temperature of 273K to the top and right edges. Convection symbols are shown.*

Verity that the custom material defined in *T4* model has thermal conductivity equal to 52.0W/m/K. Mesh the model with a default mesh and obtain a solution. Probe the **Temperature** plot at point E as shown in Figure 17-18.

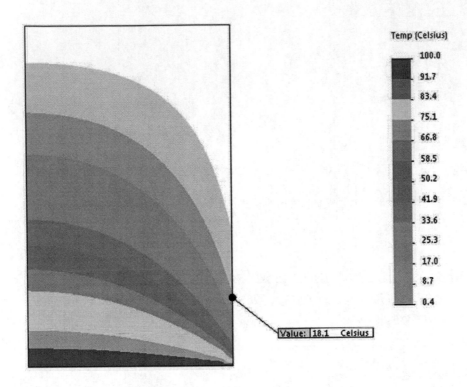

Figure 17-18: Probing temperature results in test T4.

*Probe at the intersection of the vertical edge with the horizontal split line.*

Probing shows a temperature of 18.1°C, very close to the target value of 18.3°C.

# 18: Summary and miscellaneous topics

## Topics covered

- Summary of thermal analysis exercises
- Nonlinear transient problems
- Advanced options of thermal study
- Closing remarks

As shown in the flowchart in Figure 18-1, thermal analysis may be linear or nonlinear, steady state or time dependent.

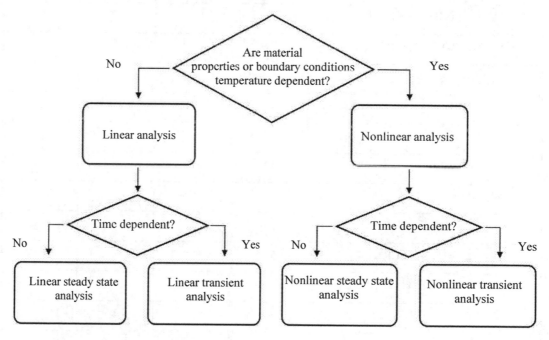

<u>Figure 18-1: Classification of thermal analysis with regard to time dependency and nonlinearity.</u>

*This is a repetition of Figure 1-12.*

In linear analyses, the conductivity matrix does not change during the solution process; in nonlinear analyses it must be modified. In steady state analyses, the boundary conditions do not change during the solution process; in time dependent (transient) analyses, boundary conditions change.

The table in Figure 18-2 classifies examples discussed in chapters 1-13 in terms of nonlinearity and time dependency.

| Chapter | Model | Linear steady state analysis | Linear transient analysis | Nonlinear steady state analysis | Nonlinear transient analysis |
|---------|-------|------------------------------|---------------------------|--------------------------------|------------------------------|
| 1 | BRACKET TH | yes | | | |
| 1 | HEAT SINK 01 | yes | | | |
| 1 | DOUBLE SYM | yes | | | |
| 1 | AXI SYM | yes | | | |
| 2 | HOLLOW PLATE TH | yes | | | |
| 3 | L BRACKET TH | yes | | | |
| 4 | STEEL ROD | yes | | | |
| 4 | TWO RODS | yes | | | |
| 5 | HEATING DUCTS | yes | | | |
| 6 | HEATING DUCTS | yes | | | |
| 7 | HOT PLATE | yes | yes | | |
| 8 | MUG | yes | yes | | |
| 9 | RECT BAR | yes | | | |
| 10 | HEAT SINK | yes | yes | | |
| 11 | GRAPHITE BALL | | | yes | |
| 12 | HEMISPHERE | | | yes | |
| 13 | BLOCKS | | | yes | |
| 16 | T2 | | | yes | |
| 16 | T3 | | yes | | |
| 16 | T4 | yes | | | |

Figure 18-2: Classification of exercises with regard to time dependency and nonlinearity.

*When "yes" appears both in steady state and transient analysis, it means that more than one study was conducted.*

All radiation problems are nonlinear because a radiation boundary condition is a function of temperature. The fact that this is temperature to the fourth power makes radiation problems strongly nonlinear. However, none of the exercises discussed so far presented a transient and nonlinear problem.

What would make a transient, nonlinear problem? This could be any radiation problem with at least one time dependent boundary condition. This could also be any transient problem with, for example, a temperature dependent material property. We will analyze both problems starting with a radiation problem which can be seen as a continuation of radiation topics presented in chapters 11, 12, 13 and 16.

Open assembly model SPACE HEATER. The model consists of an aluminum Reflector and a glass Bulb. Faces that exchange heat by radiation are indicated in Figure 18-3, Front view. The rim, and back face are assumed to be insulated. A split line on the back face (Figure 18-3, Back view) defines the position of the temperature probe. A fillet at the base of the stem is also assumed to be insulated; it won't have any boundary conditions defined. This is done to simplify calculations of view factors and this omission won't have much of an effect because of the small surface area of the fillet.

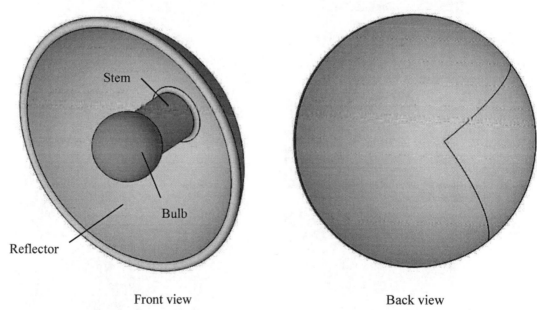

Front view                                                 Back view

Figure 18-3: SPACE HEATER assembly.

*Review this model in a section view to see that the Bulb is hollow.*

Radiation is the only mechanism of removing heat from this model. Conduction is present but heat traveling by conduction through the Bulb and Reflector is also removed by radiation. Create a **Steady State** thermal study called *01 steady state*. Define **Heat Power** and **Radiation** conditions as shown in Figures 18-4, 18-5, and 18-6.

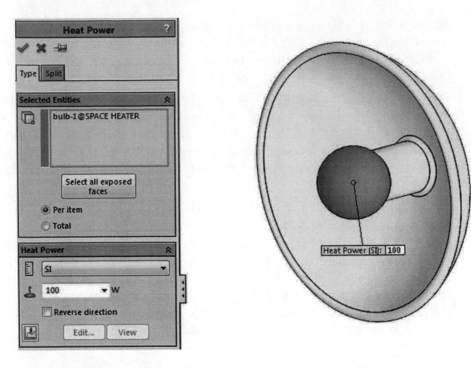

Figure 18-4: Heat power definition.

*Apply 100W to the entire Bulb; select it from the fly-out menu.*

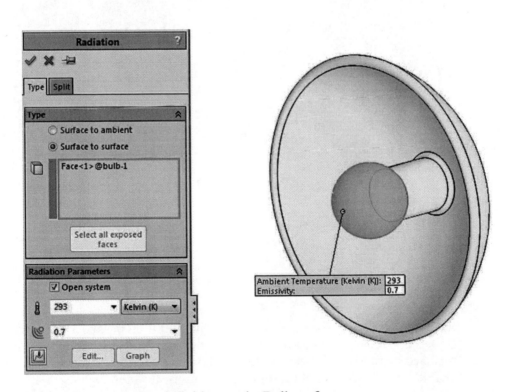

Figure 18-5: Radiation definition on the Bulb surface.

*Open system means that some heat is radiated out to space and not to the Reflector. The ambient temperature is 293K, and emissivity of Bulb surface material is 0.7.*

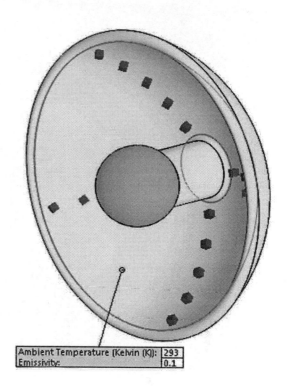

Figure 18-6: Radiation definition on Reflector surface and stem.

*Open system means that some heat is radiated out to space and not all to the Bulb. Ambient temperature is 293K, and emissivity of these faces is 0.1. Note that the Reflector is designed to reflect radiation, which is why the value of the emissivity coefficient is low.*

*The selected face is not highlighted; enlarged radiation symbols are shown.*

Mesh the assembly with the default element size, which produces a mesh barely acceptable for temperature analysis. Analysis of heat flux would definitely need a more refined mesh especially at the area of the fillet. Run the solution and review the steady state temperature as shown in Figure 18-7.

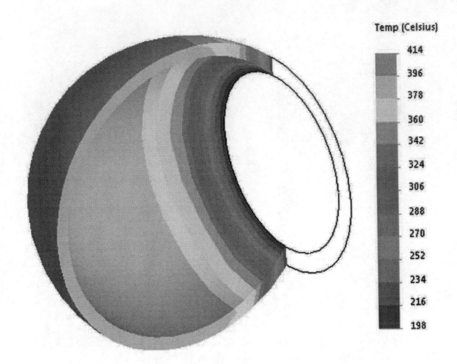

Figure 18-7: Steady state temperature results.

*This section plot is used in this illustration.*

Even though the geometry has axial symmetry, the radiation problem can't be simplified to a 2D axisymmetric model. This is because finding **View Factors** requires 3D geometry.

Notice that we have just solved nonlinear, steady state problem. We will now make it into a transient problem. Copy study *01 steady state* into *02 transient*. Define properties of the transient study as shown in Figure 18-8.

Figure 18-8: Properties of the transient thermal study.

*The duration of analysis is 1 hour covered in 10 steps at 6min intervals.*

Remember that transient thermal analysis requires an **Initial Temperature**. Define it as 298K for the entire assembly (Figure 18-9).

Figure 18-9: Definition of Initial Temperature for the assembly.

*Select the assembly from the fly-out menu. Notice that the temperature callout refers to the origin of the assembly.*

Run study *02 transient* and display the **Temperature** plot from any time step. Probe the temperature of the Bulb and Reflector, then display these temperatures as function of time; follow the steps in Figure 18-10.

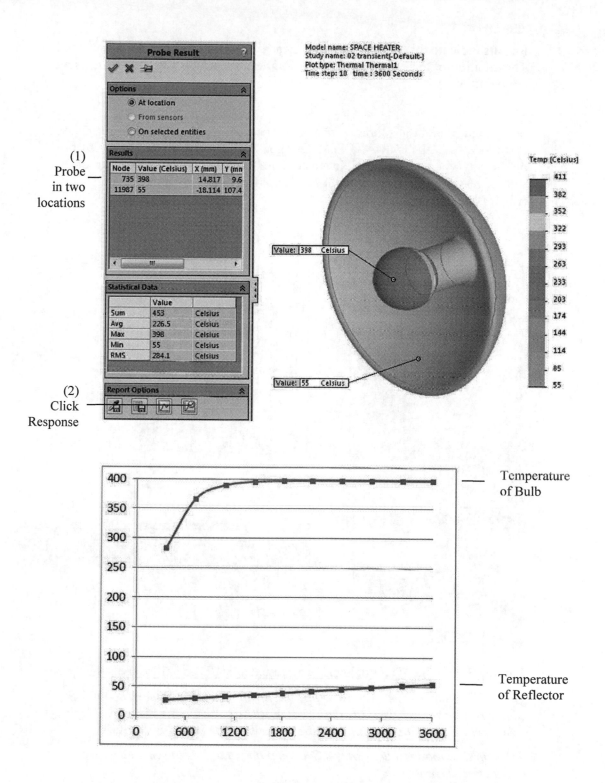

**(1) Probe in two locations**

**(2) Click Response**

Figure 18-10: Temperature of the assembly for the last step and Response graph showing temperatures in the probed location as function of time.

*The temperature of the front side of the Bulb and of the Reflector are very uniform; you may probe just about anywhere.*

Results indicate that the Bulb reaches steady state temperature after about 1500s. The duration of analysis was too short for the Reflector to reach the steady state temperature.

In the next model the source of nonlinear behavior is a material property. Open part model RADIATOR AXISYM. Our goal is to study temperature fluctuation on the ribs when a time variable temperature is applied to the end face of the stem. Create a thermal study with **2D Simplification** using axial symmetry (Figure 18-11).

Figure 18-11: The 3D model can be represented in 2D as half of the radial cross.

*Using 2D elements, we can use a fine mesh with no need for mesh control. Shown above is a mesh that used the default element size. The mesh is acceptable for temperature analysis but may require refinement for heat flux analysis.*

*2D Simplification window shows Section plane and Axis of symmetry used to create the 2D model.*

To create material with temperature dependent conductivity, first copy the material 1060 Alloy into **Custom Materials** in the **Thermal** folder, then follow the steps in Figure 18-12.

(1)
Copy material
AL1060 into
Thermal folder in
Custom materials
Name it Al temp

(2)
Use drop down arrow in
Thermal Conductivity line
to select Temperature
Dependent

(3)
Set units to °C and W/m/K.
Enter coordinates of
two points as shown

Figure 18-12: Definition of custom material with temperature dependent conductivity.

Define study properties as shown in Figure 18-13.

Figure 18-13: Definition of properties of the transient study.

*The total duration is 560s; the time increment is 4s. The analysis will be conducted in 140 steps.*

Define an Initial Temperature of 0°C as shown in Figure 18-14.

Figure 18-14: An initial temperature of 0°C is applied to the face that represents the 2D model.

*An oblique view is used to display temperature symbols.*

*An initial temperature would not be required in a steady state analysis.*

Define the time dependent temperature to the right end. The time dependency follows the equation:

$$t = 100 sin\frac{\pi t}{20} + 100 \text{ °C}.$$

This equation has been tabulated in the spreadsheet RADIATOR AXISYM.xlsx.

You may copy the table from there.

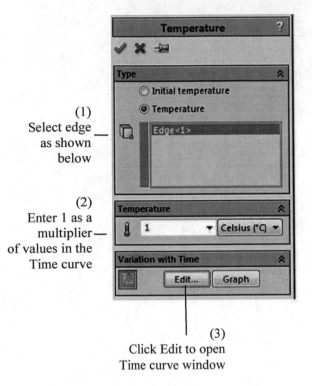

(1)
Select edge
as shown
below

(2)
Enter 1 as a
multiplier
of values in the
Time curve

(3)
Click Edit to open
Time curve window

(4)
Copy table from spreadsheet
RADIATOR AXISYM.xlsx
and paste it here, then click OK

Figure 18-15: Definition of time dependent temperature.

*These steps are similar those in Figure 13-12.*

Mesh the model with the default mesh (Figure 18-11) and obtain a solution. Display the **Temperature** plot from any step and probe results in two locations as shown in Figure 18-16.

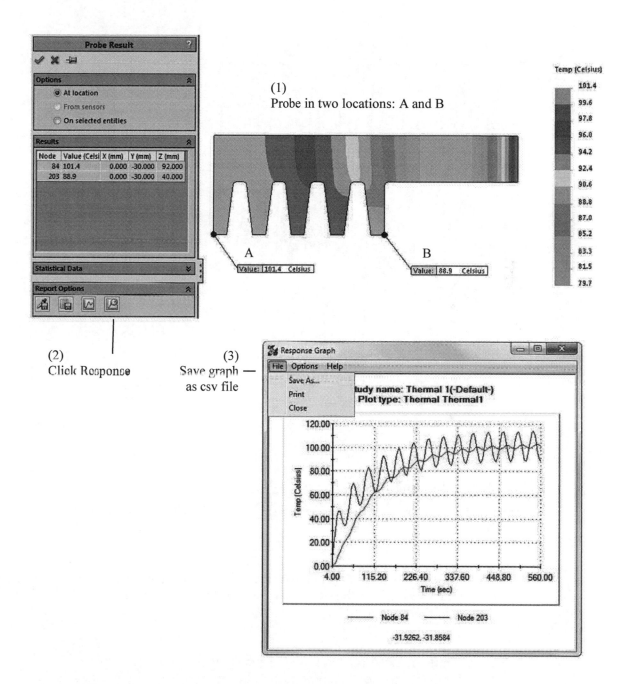

Figure 18-16: Probe temperature results in two locations as shown.

*Save the graph as a \*.csv file.*

It has been said before that graph results are easier to present using Excel which offers better graphing tools than those in **SOLIDWORKS Simulation**. The temperature in the two probed locations is shown as a function of time in Figure 18-17.

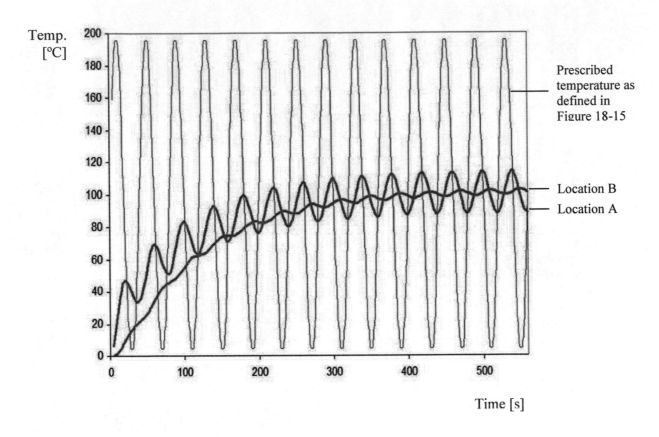

Figure 18-17: Probed temperature results in locations A and B.

*This graph also shows the prescribed temperature oscillating between 0° and 200°C.*

As we can see in Figure 18-17, temperature oscillations diminish as we move further away from where the oscillating prescribed temperature is applied. This is the effect of thermal inertia.

Notice that the RADIATOR AXISYM problem is transient and nonlinear. It solves fast thanks to the 2D representation that greatly reduces the numerical effort. Benefits of the 2D representation are particularly high when transient and/or nonlinear problems are solved.

## *Advanced options of Thermal study*

Thermal study offers **Advanced Options** that control solution of nonlinear problems (Figure 18-18).

Figure 18-18: Advanced Option in Thermal study.

*Use them to control convergence of nonlinear problem solution.*

These settings are used by the solver in a similar manner to how nonlinear solver **Advanced Options** are used in nonlinear static studies; they are particularly useful in radiation problems. For example, the Under-Relaxation Factor in Thermal **Advanced Options** is analogous to the **Singularity Elimination Factor** in **Advanced Options** of **Nonlinear** study.

## *Closing remarks*

In this book we presented a variety of heat transfer and related structural problems. Our focus was on the understanding of the physical phenomena while avoiding excessively complex models which would make solution time unnecessarily long. You will notice that the same principles and modeling techniques apply to models of any complexity.

*Notes:*

# 19: Glossary of terms

The following glossary provides short descriptions of selected terms used in this book.

**Heat**
Heat is a form of energy of a system when temperature difference exists between a system and its surroundings.

**Heat transfer**
Heat transfer is the transfer of heat energy from one system to another.

**Temperature**
Temperature is a measure of heat energy. It can be measured in K (Kelvin), °C (Celsius), and °F (Fahrenheit). Notice that the degree symbol ° is not used with K.

**Heat flux**
Heat flux is the rate of heat transfer per unit area.

**Conduction**
Conduction is a mode of heat transfer in which the heat energy is transferred on a molecular scale with no movement of macroscopic particles. Fourier's Law characterizes heat flow by conduction. The coefficient of thermal conduction characterizes heat transfer in solid bodies.

**Convection**
Convection is a mode of heat transfer between a solid face and a fluid. The movement of macroscopic particles transfers the heat energy. The convection coefficient characterizes convection between a solid body and its surrounding fluid.

**Radiation**
Radiation heat transfer occurs by means of electromagnetic waves. The heat energy can be transferred in vacuum. The Stefan-Boltzmann law characterizes radiative heat transfer.

**Linear analysis**
An analysis is linear when none of the parameters characterizing boundary conditions, material properties and loads is temperature dependent.

**Nonlinear analysis**
An analysis is nonlinear when at least one of the parameters characterizing boundary conditions, material properties or loads is temperature dependent.

**Steady state analysis**
In steady state analysis none of the parameters characterizing boundary conditions, material properties or loads is time dependent.

**Transient analysis**
An analysis is transient if at least one of the parameters characterizing boundary conditions, material properties or load is time dependent.

**Conductivity**
Conductivity characterizes heat flow per unit area in the normal direction in a solid body which takes place as a result of a temperature difference.

**Specific heat**
Specific heat is the energy required to raise the temperature of a unit of mass through a one degree Celsius (or Kelvin) temperature rise.

**Emissivity**
Emissivity is the ratio of the total energy emitted by a surface to the total energy emitted by a black surface at the same temperature.

**View factor**
View factor is a ratio of the energy reaching the second surface to the energy emitted by the first surface. If only one surface is involved and it is radiating all of its heat out, the view factor accounts for the fact that some radiation hits the same surface again before being finally radiated out to space.

**Thermal stress**
Thermal stress is stress induced in a structure as a result of non-uniform temperature distribution in the structure.

**Thermal expansion**
Thermal expansion is the tendency of matter to change in a volume in response to a change in temperature. It is described by a coefficient of thermal expansion.

# 20: References

This textbook builds on an understanding of structural analysis with the Finite Element Method and assumes familiarity with structural and introductory thermal analysis to the extent of the textbook (1).

To review fundamentals of Heat Transfer and fundamentals of the Finite Element Method, readers are referred to the following literature listed here in the order of relevance.

1. Kurowski P. "Engineering Analysis with SOLIDWORKS Simulation 2014," SDC Publications 2015

2. NAFEMS Background to Benchmarks, NAFEMS 1993

3. How to undertake Finite Element Based Thermal Analysis NAFEMS 2002

4. Incropera F., Dewitt D., Bergman T., Lavine A. "Fundamentals of Heat and Mass Transfer," John Wiley & Sons, Inc., 2006

5. Logan D. "A First Course in the Finite Element Method," Brooks/Cole 2007

The full list of NAFEMS publications can be found at www.nafems.org. Another internet site with a number of FEA related publications is presented by Design Generator Inc. Publications related to FEA fundamentals, training, and implementation can be found at: **www.designgenerator.com/publications.htm**

# 21: List of exercises

| Chapter | Part | Assembly | Spreadsheet |
|---|---|---|---|
| 1 | BRACKET TH<br>HEAT SINK 01<br>DOUBLE SYM<br>AXI SYM | | |
| 2 | HOLLOW PLATE TH | | |
| 3 | L BRACKET TH | | |
| 4 | STEEL ROD | TWO RODS | |
| 5 | | HEATING DUCTS | |
| 6 | | HEATING DUCTS | |
| 7 | | HOT PLATE | |
| 8 | MUG | | |
| 9 | RECT BAR | | |
| 10 | | HEAT SINK TH | HEAT SINK TH |
| 11 | GRAPHITE BALL | | |
| 12 | HEMISPHERE | | |
| 13 | | BLOCKS | |
| 14 | | ELBOW<br>MANIFOLD | |
| 15 | | INTERNAL FLOW<br>EXTERNAL FLOW<br>BALL15 | |
| 16 | | RADIATIVE HEAT<br>TRANSFER | |
| 17 | T2<br>T3<br>T4 | | T3 |
| 18 | RADIATOR AXISYM<br>RADIATOR 2015* | SPACE HEATER | RADIATOR AXISYM |

\* This is the cover page model; it comes with Simulation studies defined.

# Analysis of Machine Elements Using SOLIDWORKS Simulation 2015

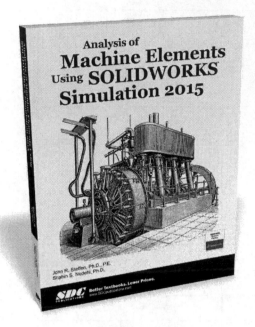

*John R. Steffen Ph.D., P.E.*
*450 Pages     ISBN 978-1-58503-929-6*
*Beginner*

- Designed for first-time SOLIDWORKS Simulation 2015 users
- Focuses on examples commonly found in Design of Machine Elements courses
- Problems are accompanied by solutions using classical equations
- Combines step-by-step tutorials with detailed explanations of why each step is taken
- Includes a chapter on design optimization

This textbook is written primarily for first-time SOLIDWORKS Simulation 2015 users who wish to understand finite element analysis capabilities applicable to stress analysis of mechanical elements. The focus of examples is on problems commonly found in an introductory, undergraduate, Design of Machine Elements or similarly named courses.

In order to be compatible with most machine design textbooks, this text begins with problems that can be solved with a basic understanding of mechanics of materials. Problem types quickly migrate to include states of stress found in more specialized situations common to a design of mechanical elements course.

# An Introduction to SOLIDWORKS Flow Simulation 2015

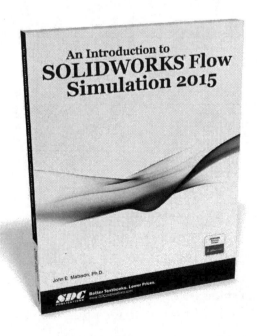

*John E. Matsson Ph.D.*
*350 Pages     ISBN 978-1-58503-934-0*
*Beginner - Intermediate*

- Step-by-step tutorials cover the creation of parts, setup and calculations with SOLIDWORKS Flow Simulation
- Covers fluid mechanics, fluid flow and heat transfer simulations
- Results are compared to analytical solutions and empirical data
- Features a chapter on Flow Past a Model Rocket

This textbook takes you through the steps of creating the SOLIDWORKS part for the simulation followed by the setup and calculation of the SOLIDWORKS Flow Simulation project. The results from calculations are visualized and compared with theoretical solutions and empirical data. Each chapter starts with the objectives and a description of the specific problems that are studied.

This book is intended to be a supplement to undergraduate Fluid Mechanics and Heat Transfer related courses. This book can also be used to show students the capabilities of fluid flow and heat transfer simulations in freshman and sophomore courses. Both internal and external flow problems are covered and compared with experimental results and analytical solutions.

# Engineering Statics Labs with SOLIDWORKS Motion 2015

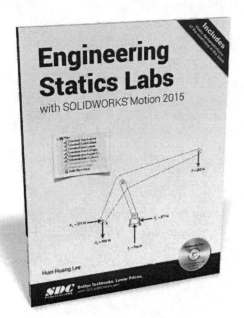

Huei-Huang Lee
160 Pages      ISBN 978-1-58503-941-8
Beginner - Intermediate

- Designed to complement a standard statics textbook
- Aids students in learning engineering ideas, concepts, and formulas
- Uses easy to understand, step-by-step instructions
- Comes with a concise introduction to SOLIDWORKS ebook in PDF format
- Includes video demonstrations of every section of the book

This book is designed as a software-based lab book to complement a standard textbook in an engineering statics course, which is usually taught at the undergraduate level. This book can also be used as an auxiliary workbook in a CAE or Finite Element Analysis course for undergraduate students.

This textbook has been carefully developed with the understanding that CAE software has developed to a point that it can be used as a tool to aid students in learning engineering ideas, concepts and even formulas. These concepts are demonstrated in each section of this book. Using the graphics-based tools of SOLIDWORKS Motion can help reduce the dependency on mathematics to teach these concepts substantially. The contents of this book have been written to match the contents of most statics textbooks.

# Mechanics of Materials Labs with SOLIDWORKS Simulation 2015

Huei-Huang Lee
300 Pages      ISBN 978-1-58503-937-1
Beginner - Intermediate

- Designed to complement a standard mechanics of materials textbook
- Aids students in learning engineering ideas, concepts, and formulas
- Uses easy to understand, step-by-step instructions
- Comes with a concise introduction to SOLIDWORKS ebook in PDF format
- Includes video demonstrations of every section of the book

# Engineering Dynamics Labs with SOLIDWORKS Motion 2015

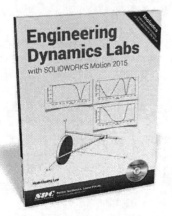

Huei-Huang Lee
250 Pages      ISBN 978-1-58503-935-7
Beginner - Intermediate

- Designed to complement a standard engineering dynamics textbook
- Aids students in learning engineering ideas, concepts, and formulas
- Uses easy to understand, step-by-step instructions
- Comes with a concise introduction to SOLIDWORKS eBook in PDF format
- Includes video demonstrations of every section of the book

# Vibration Analysis with SOLIDWORKS Simulation 2015

Paul M. Kurowski
*300 Pages     ISBN 978-1-58503-938-8*
*Intermediate - Advanced*

- Introduces you to both vibration analysis and its implementation in SOLIDWORKS Simulation 2015
- Covers all types of vibration analysis available in SOLIDWORKS Simulation
- Uses hands on exercises that build on one another throughout the book
- Designed for users already familiar with Finite Element Analysis using SOLIDWORKS Simulation

Vibration Analysis with SOLIDWORKS Simulation 2015 goes beyond the standard software manual. It concurrently introduces the reader to vibration analysis and its implementation in SOLIDWORKS Simulation using hands-on exercises. A number of projects are presented to illustrate vibration analysis and related topics. Each chapter is designed to build on the skills and understanding gained from previous exercises.

Vibration Analysis with SOLIDWORKS Simulation 2015 is designed for users who are already familiar with the basics of Finite Element Analysis (FEA) using SOLIDWORKS Simulation or who have completed the book Engineering Analysis with SOLIDWORKS Simulation 2015.

# Engineering Analysis with SOLIDWORKS Simulation 2015

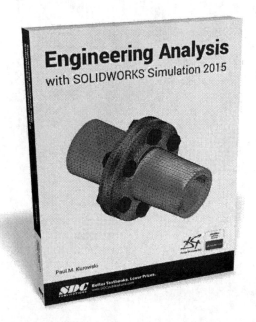

Paul M. Kurowski
*500 Pages     ISBN 978-1-58503-933-3*
*Beginner - Intermediate*

- Concurrently introduces SOLIDWORKS Simulation & Finite Element Analysis
- Covers a wide variety of Finite Element Analysis problems
- Uses hands-on exercises that build on one another throughout the book

Engineering Analysis with SOLIDWORKS Simulation 2015 goes beyond the standard software manual. Its unique approach concurrently introduces you to the SOLIDWORKS Simulation 2015 software and the fundamentals of Finite Element Analysis (FEA) through hands-on exercises. A number of projects are presented using commonly used parts to illustrate the analysis features of SOLIDWORKS Simulation. Each chapter is designed to build on the skills, experiences and understanding gained from the previous chapters.

Topics covered include: linear static analysis of parts and assemblies, contact stress analysis, frequency (modal) analysis, buckling analysis, thermal analysis, drop test analysis, nonlinear analysis, dynamic analysis, random vibration analysis, h and p adaptive solution methods, modeling techniques, Implementation of FEA in the design process and much more.